How to Apply
to Graduate School
Without Really Lying

How to Apply to Graduate School Without Really Lying

Charles Walters

Nelson-Hall nh Chicago

Library of Congress Cataloging in Publication Data

Walters, Charles.
    How to apply to graduate school without really
lying.

    Bibliography: p.
    Includes index.
    1.   Universities and colleges — United States —
Graduate work.   2.   Universities and colleges — United
States — Entrance requirements.   I.   Title.
LB2371.W29   378.1′05′7   79-19988
ISBN 0-88229-537-3 (cloth)
ISBN 0-88229-744-9 (paper)

Manufactured in the United States of America

10   9   8   7   6   5   4   3   2   1

To Academia.
Without it this book
never would have been written.

Contents

Preface

This is an incomplete preface. It only describes who I imagined you to be as I wrote this book and what's in it for you. I'll tell you why I wrote it later.

I thought of you as one of my undergraduate advisees. I wrote much as I talk when one of them first asks me how to apply to graduate school. I've never said quite this much to any one advisee but it's been building up in me for years. Now I've said it all. Well, almost all.

Once or twice it did cross my mind that a faculty colleague might recommend this book to one of his advisees. If your advisor has done that, listen to all the *other* advice he gives you as well. Anyone's advice might not turn out to be perfect in a particular case but your advisor is a realist. That's important; eyes open is better than eyes closed any day.

Most self-help books try to convince you that you are better than you think you are. I won't do that because I have no idea whether or not it's true; nor will you as a result of reading this book, as far as I know.

Anyway, whether you are or aren't better than you think is irrelevant. What matters in applying to graduate school is whether certain academicians think you're better than some number of other applicants.

The main point of this book is to describe how you can convince those academic decision-makers that you are exactly the sort of student they want. When you've done that they'll invite you in and pay you money while you're there. The most amazing things have been known to result from a well-managed application campaign.

This all has to do with something social psychologists call impression management. I've given you many specific directions for managing your academic impression.

All principles of impression management would be of little use to you without a realistic description of the semi-mad process of graduate school application. Some candid descriptions of academicians, their norms, and their pressure points are also necessary if you are to use these principles to get what you want. These things, too, I've provided you, even though a less than idealized (but, I think, understandably human) portrait of Academia results.

I've also told you how to find the information you need to locate programs in all academic fields, to find details about any, to learn the interests of the faculty in those programs, to discover the reputation of any given department, and other things of that sort.

Last, I've given you specific plans to follow in arranging to get strong letters of recommendation, how to write effective descriptions of your own interests and study plans, and some facts about financial aid that are usually not known to undergraduates.

So, imagine that I'm sitting in my rather conventionally furnished office and you've asked my advice about how to apply to graduate school.

Here goes. . .

ONE
Inside the
Hallowed Halls

You may have spent your money for this book for any number of reasons. One certainty, though, is that facing the prospect of applying to graduate school provokes anxiety in everyone who does it.

You are *not* different because you are unsure about what to do first, how to find out what schools you should consider, or, even, in what particular field you should plan to study. Everyone who is thinking about applying — no matter what their academic record — feels the same way you do. Some people are just more willing to admit it than others.

Why shouldn't you be anxious? You've never done it before. It seems to you to be extremely important that you make the "correct" decision. And, it's not very clear how you go about getting the information you need. Who wouldn't be anxious under those circumstances?

I'm a working academician (a psychologist, as it happens) and I've been on the faculty of a university for over a dozen years. Not only do I remember my own state of mind when I applied to graduate school, I've seen scores of undergraduates trying to cope as best they could with the very situation you face. I've also read hundreds of applications for graduate study at my own university so I've seen what the absence of realistic advice can do to what might have been an otherwise promising applicant.

Thousands of applicants muddle through on their own each year, and large numbers fail to make it into some graduate school. Even bright and highly motivated students fail to make it into some graduate school. I've often wondered how many of them didn't make it because they had not had realistic advice from someone who knows what it's like on the inside. Even though I'll never know the answer to this question, I have decided to do something about making realistic advice available to those who want to go to graduate school.

This book contains specific, practical directions that you can use to maximize your chances of getting in. I can assure you that my advice will not only help you, you will be surprised by some of the recommendations I will make.

Some of the things I'll say in this book will sound cynical to you. I cannot help that. All I can do is assure you that I am describing the way it is in what I think of as plain, candid language. I am on your side and I believe you are due the truth as I see it. Others may see it differently than I. I say let them write their own books.

I'll assume, of course, that you are highly motivated to get into graduate school. Within broad limits, your academic record is much less important to either getting in or doing well than is your motivation to work at what you're doing. If you want it and will work at it, you'll profit by taking my advice. Remember always that the people who will be new graduate students next year are many of the same people with whom you partied, lived, and blew grass in your undergraduate years. They are not beings from another planet; they could be you — one year from now.

As one sample of what I know to be true and you almost surely do not, I can assure you that many, many students become graduate students who would never themselves have believed that their undergraduate records would suffice.

The reason is plain. Graduate departments *must* accept some number of new students each year or lose the primary justification for their continued existence. That justification is the training of graduate students, of course. Beyond that, in some fields (e.g., chemistry) the department could not operate its undergraduate program if it did not have graduate students to act as laboratory course assistants.

Think about that for a moment! Some number of new students must be accepted each year. It may not seem possible but there are about two hundred-fifty different Ph.D. *specialities* listed in the annual survey of doctoral recipients conducted by the National Research Council. Moreover, in psychology alone there are over four hundred degree-granting (i.e., M.A., Ph.D., or both) *departments* in the United States. That means there are a lot of bodies that must be found each year if these multitudes of graduate programs are not to founder for lack of customers or cheap labor.

Those statistics may even cause you to wonder if you need this primer on applying. If so, don't. You do. Or, at least almost all of you can help yourselves in some significant way by reading the lessons it contains. For the past dozen years I have seen the evidence for this conclusion in the sixty to seventy applications per year I've read from applicants in social psychology at my own university. The same mistakes appear again and again. The same omissions are apparent to the educated eye. Both can be avoided if you know what to do.

I've said I'll be candid so now it's time to be candid about myself. My own reasons for writing this book are simply described.

First, I'm convinced that there are large numbers of undergraduates who yearn for graduate school but mistakenly believe their records are too weak for that to be possible. If some of these people are truly not qualified, that's one thing. However, if qualified people are not discovered merely because they didn't have realistic advice about how to apply, that's another matter altogether. Those are the people I want to reach.

Second, I'm a social psychologist who has spent a good part of his career reading about, thinking about, and practicing *impression management*. These are the acts of appearing to be the person you want to be. I am, therefore, intrigued by the endless possibilities of applying what I know about this mixture of art and science to the practical problems you'll face in gaining access to a graduate school. No matter how much you already know about impression management yourself, you can't do your best without my advice because you don't have accurate information about Academia or the denizens who dwell there. You may some day but you haven't it now—when you need it.

Last, after living the life for years, I'm able to give you a perspective on Academia that is ordinarily quite unavailable to outsiders. In fact, insiders simply do not discuss with outsiders the matters I will discuss.

Indeed, as I write this, I fully anticipate more than a few raised eyebrows if it is learned that I've discussed them. I said I'd be candid but I didn't say I was crazy. That's why I've used a pseudonym rather than my own name as author. To my knowledge, there is no person named Charles Walters. At least, if there is, he's not the person writing this book. Maybe I'm not even a he.

To sum it up, I believe you have something I need (an audience) and I have something you need (realistic advice). I hope you'll agree some day that it was a fair exchange.

Let Confidence Be Your Shield

No matter how specific my advice, I cannot know the details of your particular circumstances. You must adapt my lessons and illustrations to your circumstances for yourself. I'm here to help you but I cannot apply for you. Still, with my advice in mind, you'll have an enormous advantage over your peers who are struggling along on the basis of bits and pieces of information offered by friends, parents, and the occasional sympathetic advisor.

The most troublesome attitude you'll have to overcome is that you are somehow "not good enough" to go to graduate school. Almost every student falls prey to this self doubt. It doesn't make any difference what the academic record has been, either. At one time or another (and with some it's a chronic state), you'll think about what will happen to you if it turns out that you don't *get in*.

My advice on this point is, I know, easier to give than to take, but so is almost all advice. As a realist, I counsel realism, of course. And, in this regard, realism is to recognize that when you have done all you can to take your best shot, what happens then—happens.

At some point the decision on your application will be made at a meeting of two to ten faculty members in the area to which you've applied for graduate study. There are many things you can do before that meeting to markedly increase the odds on a favorable decision on your application. That's what this book is about, after all. But after you've done those things, it's out of your hands. Worry seldom accomplishes anything except raising ulcers.

Principles of Impression Management

Every human being who has managed to stay alive in our society has some, however imperfect, working grasp of these principles. You are a human being and are alive. Therefore, you already have a working grasp of these principles. Perhaps you'd rather not brag about that fact or, even, admit it but I hope we will come to be candid with one another and accept that we both know it to be true.

But, having a "working grasp" of the following principles in *familiar* social situations is one thing. Having explicit, clear knowledge of each one and realizing that they are fully applicable in *unfamiliar* social situations is another thing altogether. That you may not have—yet.

In one way or another, all the advice I'll have for you is based on some one or another of the *principles of impression management* I'm about to make explicit for you. You must study these principles if you are to learn to think creatively about the unfamiliar social situation you face in applying yourself. That is, after all, what the system is: an unfamiliar (to you) social situation. Happily, it is not unfamiliar to me and I will guide you. But, I cannot be with you, so remember, to the daring and subtle go the spoils. If that fact is unacceptable to you, your best bet is to have long ago arranged to be born of wealthy parents.

Principle 1

Audience segregation is the rock on which successful impression management is founded. If two *gatekeepers* (see Glossary) need you to be two different persons for reasons of your own, you can give them what they need as long as they don't compare notes.

You surely have been a different individual to your parents and your peers for a number of years. Both they and you have needed that difference so you've provided it. Obviously, as long as your parents and peers never get together for a chat about the "real" you, you'll continue to satisfy their needs as well as your own.

There is no "real" you. There is no "real" me. There are only the persons that are experienced. And, in most cases, an audience of Segregated Others is an audience untroubled by counterproductive concerns with "reality."

Principle 2

Inside knowledge is the key to successful impression management. A gatekeeper who doesn't expect you to know as much as you know is in for a number of pleasant surprises.

We all reach conclusions about other individuals based on what we expect of "people like them." While you are applying yourself, the people "like you" are others who are applying to graduate school.

If you do no more than read this book, you'll know more than your compatriots-in-application. If nothing else, you'll be able to provide your gatekeepers with a number of pleasant surprises by simply *knowing the score* (see Glossary).

If you follow my advice in your own application campaign, you'll get all the personal credit because your gatekeepers have no way of knowing that your actions are based on inside information.

Principle 3

Credibility once lost, like virginity, is never regained. To attempt to appear the perfect young scientist, scholar, or artist is to risk alerting your gatekeepers that all is not as it seems to be. Your management of the impression you convey will depend on your gatekeepers suspending disbelief in many matters large and small. Do not risk your credibility on minor matters.

No one is perfect. No one actually reads every word on the editorial page every day, remembers every word from every lecture, or has read every important book published in the last ten years. And no one—especially an academician—enjoys the experience of being thought naive. Don't risk suggesting that thought for the sake of making only a few small points.

Principle 4

Effortful impression management is bad impression management. If it looks as if you're working hard at it, you're probably wasting your time.

In fact, an effective application campaign takes considerable work. The point here is to let only as much of that work show as is necessary to manage the intended impression. It is partly because the work that goes into the preparation is invisible that the campaign has such positive impact.

Would you object if a gatekeeper thought of you, "He just seems to do all the right things without being told"? I should think not!

Principle 5

Simple messages are the marks of successful impression management. Your gatekeepers must see the message themselves without you having to draw a diagram for them.

While in the presence of gatekeepers, your attention must seem to be focused entirely on the academic business at hand. You may be asking for a letter of reference, arranging for an independent study course, or any number of other things. That is why you are there but, of course, that's not the only reason you're there. It is in that other reason, the management of the impression you want to convey, that there must be simple messages about the sort of person you need to be.

This brings me to a question that may be on your mind. You may have asked yourself whether there isn't something underhanded about this business of impression management. I've told you I'll be candid with you so here's what I think about that. If you disagree, I hope it's because you've thought about it and are not reacting emotionally.

It's been said that the impression manager differs from someone who is behaving "naturally" by seeming to focus on the *present* interaction while actually focusing on *future* benefits. Perhaps so.

However, it's concluded from this that since the other person who's behaving "naturally" hasn't been warned of this, it's sneaky for the impression manager to behave like that. Nonsense.

That is, it's nonsense unless we're talking about "naturally" behaving children or people who've drunk too much alcohol in the last few hours. For anyone else, it's nonsense.

All but children and drunks have the same working grasp of the principles of impression management that have been learned by any intact human being in our society. None such requires any further instruction in the fact that *all* social interactions are complex bundles of information exchange, impression management, and affective recreation.

In short, I believe that "natural" social behavior is a complex bundle, that everyone knows it, and that there is nothing sneaky about acting on that fact. It is simplistic to imagine otherwise. It is also unrealistic.

Principle 6

Gullibility is not a sometime thing. In Academia, it's everywhere. You can depend on it throughout your application campaign.

Gullibility is not stupidity. Academicians are, in general, not stupid. This fact is important to you because if they were stupid you'd have to draw diagrams (see Principle 5). They are quick to draw inferences (i.e., not stupid) from unobtrusive information but slow to consider (i.e., gullible) that the information has, itself, been created for that purpose.

I believe that their characteristic gullibility traces to the constant repetitions of the norm of scholarship that I'll describe in more detail shortly. The essence of this norm (or, rule of ideal behavior) is that all evidence must be accurately reported no matter how much it hurts. They were told by their own teachers and, in turn, have told their own students that this is the norm in Academia so many times that they tend to overgeneralize it as applying to evidence of any kind.

Consequently, they don't stop to consider that, at most, this norm applies to scholarly evidence which is subject to constant reexamination by other academicians who will benefit by discovering a mistake! They act, then, as if evidence is evidence — even the evidence you display to them in the course of your application campaign.

The Way It Is

In the absence of certain knowledge about graduate programs and their gatekeeper inhabitants, you cannot apply these principles of impression management to their full potential. Providing you with that knowledge will be one of the more useful things I hope to do for you in this book.

Still, I don't want to give you the idea that Academia is inhabited by worthless people, or that you'll not find innumerable satisfactions in being a part of it. I have, and *all* of my best friends are academicians. But I've assured you of straight talk (as *I* see it, remember) and I assume you want that or you wouldn't still be reading. Keep in mind that in singling out academicians and Academia, I'm saying little other than what I believe applies to all human beings and institutions.

If the graduate application system were really what it appears to be to an outsider, many strategies based on the principles of impression management would be fruitless. The system is not, however, objective, equitable, or operated to actually insure the collection of valid information. In fact, if the system were this way, you might very well be stuck with revealing the whole truth about yourself.

When the realities of application to a graduate school are viewed with the eye of an insider, the difference between *what seems to be* and *what is* appears absurd. It is absurd.

The only thing that maintains the semicorrespondence between the *ideal* and the *real* are the actions of applicants as they submit to the norm of candor as well as their own false beliefs about penalities for violating this norm. I needn't say much about candor norms. You've surely heard that Honesty Is the Best Policy and that Crime Doesn't Pay. What I may be able to help you correct are your false beliefs about violating this norm while applying to graduate school.

To that end, please consider that the administration of penalities of *any* kind for anything depends on some enforcement agent discovering that some norm, rule, or law has been violated. Application to graduate school is not like seeking a job with the Central Intelligence Agency. Moreover, you are not even dealing with gatekeepers who will exercise the slight suspicion about your *credential claims* (see Glossary) that would be customary if you were buying a $20 watch on credit. Practically everything will be taken at something fairly close to face value—if your gate-keepers want to assist you or accept you. And, getting them to want to do that is only partly dependent on your academic record. Indeed, I believe there are grounds for supposing that your academic record may be the lesser part but no one knows this for sure.

There are, of course, a few elementary *validity checks* (see Glossary) by those agencies that supply certain parts of your credentials (e.g., official transcripts, Graduate Record Exams (GREs), Miller Analogies Tests (MATs), and so on). I'll refer to these parts as your *hard credentials* (see Glossary) and there is little you can do about the numbers on them (except study, of course).

There are, however, several things you can do about the meaning that's attributed to those numbers by your gate-keepers. People have been ill on the day their GREs were given, and it is believed by many academicians that some students suffer from chronic test anxiety which interferes with their "true" performance, and freshmen who get low grades do "find themselves." And, of course, the individual whose poverty made it necessary to work and whose fighting spirit made it possible to graduate has been known to be given some understanding for his lowish grades. None of your gatekeepers will be aware of such special circumstances unless you somehow let them know, obviously. But there are some ways that are better than others for doing so. That, too, is what this book is about.

For your *soft credentials* (see Glossary), there are no validity checks. These credentials (e.g., letters of recommendation and an autobiographical statement, chiefly) are not only unchecked, they regularly command inordinate weight in the decision that will be made (or, not made) in your favor. This is particularly astonishing, since, for example, letters of recommendation are typically written by people you choose, people who know what you want them to know about you, and (at the same time) people who haven't the opportunity to assess the validity of their knowledge of you.

Similarly, your written statement about your past and future interests that is a standard part of graduate applications is even more firmly under your control. Assuming you will have access to inside information about the gatekeepers who will read it, it would be quite surprising if this statement could not be made to sound very attractive to those for whom it is written.

In short, as concerns your *hard credentials* to some extent and your *soft credentials* to a near maximum extent, where is the enforcement agent who could possibly know that you have or have not fully submitted to the norm of candor? There's no effective enforcement agent in practice. There simply isn't one!

Now you know why I said the difference between the *ideal* and the *real* is absurd.

Beyond that, even if there were effective enforcement agents for candor violations, penalty administration depends on *clear* evidence of such violations. If one of the reasons you are admitted is that some third party attested to your maturity and motivation, who is to say you are responsible if that turns out to be a poor judgment? Similarly, if you are admitted because of your expressed love for a certain type of research, who is to say that more recent experiences have not resulted in an honest change of view? Where would there be any clear evidence of violation of a norm of candor? There'd be none!

The gist of this point is that no matter what you might

have thought, you are faced with managing your impression for gatekeepers who are surprisingly tolerant of your reinterpretations of numbers from the past or who have no means of judging the validity of important parts of your credentials. Since I assume you believe you're qualified for graduate school, I'll assume you agree that everyone will be glad to have you there, once they see what you can do. Why, then, should you allow your qualifications to be overlooked because some pieces of paper are allowed to speak for themselves?

The Norms of Academia

The last topic of general orientation I'll discuss is one concerning the self-perceptions of academicians and the closely coupled norms to which they subscribe. This discussion will also give me a chance to tell you about some realities of graduate school education although I'll save the one having to do primarily with money for a later chapter.

You must have a realistic idea of the target of your impression management. The rifleman may be very skillful but if he's shooting in the dark he'll hit few bull's eyes.

Along with all other human beings, academicians take themselves and their norms (i.e., ideal rules of behavior) very, very seriously. They do joke among one another about the sloppy research in their journals and the gamesmanship of survival in the academic world. However, these displays of humor are *strictly* for other *clubpersons* (see Glossary) and are not thought the slightest bit funny when coming from a nonclubperson.

Since the successful management of your impression will depend on appearing to personify (within reason) the values expressed by these self-perceptions and norms, you must know what they are. I'm not asking that you approve of them or, even, that you now accept them as your own. I am warning you, though, that if your impression isn't managed to make you appear to accept them, you'll put your own application campaign in grave jeopardy.

Norm 1

The use of the best methods is its own reward.

An academician views himself as one who personifies the values of craftsmanship in his research, writing, or teaching. Whether he be physiologist, historian, or psychologist, he will sing the pleasures of doing his own work cleanly and appreciation of the work of others produced with similar rigor.

By and large, any academician's standard for judging cleanly done work is simple. It is work that is done as *his* teachers did it or work that is done as *he* and his academic allies do it. That there may be enormous differences between his style of work and others who also call themselves physiologists, historians, or psychologists is not relevant. Any academician likes his way best. Beyond that, he may even believe that there is no other way that is half as good.

What is important for you to realize is that an academician will recognize a kindred spirit in you if you simply share his ideas about the importance of using the best methods in your work. The inside information I'll tell you how to collect later will simplify your problem of knowing which are the best methods as concerns a given gatekeeper.

Norm 2

The accumulation of knowledge is its own reward.

The times are changing but Academia is still inhabited by a large majority of individuals who subscribe to this norm. Even those who are in what might be called the more "applied" academic specialities still accept this norm although they are careful not to admit it in their own research grant applications. Everyone knows which side federal grants are buttered on, and granting agencies have moved effectively by the oldest method known toward reconstructing graduate programs with explicit emphasis on *applications* of knowledge.

The English infantryman had a saying for it. "If you take the Queen's shilling, you must do the Queen's bidding." Graduate schools began taking (with both hands) federal grant money for research and student support in the late forties. The growth of graduate programs climbed as a result through the fifties. In the sixties this growth took off like a rocket. The federal money flowed like wine at a festival. In the early seventies, the Feds (as government agencies are called collectively) cut back sharply on the dollar flow to universities in general and graduate programs in particular.

The graduate programs have outgrown the capacity (or willingness) of state governments to support them. The Feds have begun to put on their Queen costumes and made it clear that the time to take orders has come.

Of course, the Feds don't call it "giving orders" but no realist can mistake it for what it is. The rallying cries of legislators are accountability, sunset doctoral programs, and market demand. The lure is the continuation of *some* federal monies. The disclaimers of intent to control graduate education are such statements as, "I am by no means calling for greater government involvement in the internal affairs of graduate education, but rather for greater accountability as to how the taxpayer's dollar is spent."

The watchword of a realist is that if two things come down to the same thing, there is no difference between the two things. No matter *what* the Queen may say.

What all this means for your application campaign is that you may easily mistake the cries of the times for the norms of the gatekeepers whom you will face. It may be that fifteen years from now most academicians will agree with legislators that graduate school training must be continually adjusted to the nation's needs for engineers, accountants, historians, political scientists, and zoologists. But, most academicians don't accept that now. They were schooled five to thirty-five years ago. Then it was believed that graduate students were preparing to continue the process of knowledge accumulation. Your gatekeepers, in general, do recognize that things are changing. But, they don't like it! And, they don't really care much for people who do like it. You should avoid appearing to be one of those people. After you're in graduate school you can take another look at the question.

Norm 3

The evergreen process of free dissemination of knowledge links today's academician with the past and the future.

An academician wants very much to perceive himself as an intellectual, artistic, or scientific agent who acts on the work of those who have come before him and transmits something of himself to those who come after him.

Most recognize that the Einsteins, Hemingways, and Dalis are few and far between. Still, most academicians begin their own careers with the secret thought in mind that, perhaps, they too will achieve that sort of eminence. And, of course, most of them do not.

Even though they may come eventually to reckon with their own shortfalls — as the larger world may view it — they can still take some comfort in the thought that, perhaps, one of their own students may make it. And, if not, then perhaps a student of one of their own students. There is always that hope, isn't there?

As to your application campaign, then, tread carefully

when you are tempted to suggest that all who have come
before you were patent idiots without your insight into the
fundamental problems of your field.

You may think it will make you more attractive to
display your clever judgments on these points. But, remember, one of those who has come before you is the
academician who is reading (or listening to) your New
Manifesto. He is not likely to be favorably impressed by
your criticism. And, *he* will assist in deciding on your acceptance to graduate school.

Norm 4

In decisions relating to an academic speciality the last
word should be heard from the specialists.

As far as you're concerned this norm comes down to
considerable deference being accorded those specialists in
the *sub-area* (see Glossary) to which you apply for study by
their colleagues on faculty committees.

This does not necessarily mean that these sub-area faculty
will always have the final say about admitting you if that
involves giving you some form of financial support in your
first year. Even if the decision doesn't involve financial
support for you in the first year, there may be some restriction on the number of admittees for any of several reasons.
Some limit on available facilities and the prospect of the
need for later financial support are the two most prominent of these reasons.

Still, academicians are accustomed to letting those "in" a
sub-area make admissions decisions just as they make decisions about proposals for new courses or other business
thought internal to the sub-area in question.

The norm would be defended on the ground that these
are the people best informed and, so, they should be the
ones to make "internal" decisions.

It is because of this norm that my later advice will again and again draw your attention to the importance of properly managing your impression with gatekeepers in or close to the sub-area to which you're applying. In general, their opinions, whether as letter writers or readers, are likely to have the greatest impact on the committee decision to admit or not admit you.

Norm 5

Research activity of some kind is the single most important indicator of being academically alive.

In almost all universities and some colleges this norm is translated into the question of how much has been published, lately. In most colleges, particularly those that publically assure everyone that they are oriented toward teaching, there are less clear-cut standards for research activity. Still, even in these teaching colleges, a faculty member who doesn't show regular signs of reading (at least) in his field will likely be thought of as dead wood by his colleagues.

This reading is called "keeping up with the literature" and keeping up is impossible to do in even the very narrowest of sub-areas. There is simply too much information (or what passes for it until examined) in too many journals, monographs, and books. This is one reason for the chronic guilt I believe most academicians feel. They not only can't keep up with the literature in their own field, they know they are continually falling behind no matter how hard they try. Most eventually become realists about it and simply do the best they can.

What this means for your application campaign is that in almost all academic specialities (and even some professional ones), it should seem that research of some kind should be indicated as your first priority. Even if you plan to work in a setting having nothing to do a university or college, remember that graduate school gatekeepers subscribe to this norm. As does any human being, they believe people similar to themselves are understandable. And, you do want them to understand you, don't you?

An Encouraging Word

Now that you've these principles and norms in mind, you're ready to get down to specifics. I can't know your particular circumstances so I've tried to cover the things that will be useful to anyone who is applying.

You may soon find yourself wondering whether I'm dwelling on nitpicking detail that you won't need to know about to get in. I think that even if you decide not to actually do some of these things, your eyes will be opened a little wider to reality by reading about them.

Also, you should think about this rule-of-thumb from the advertising business: fifty percent of what you do to promote a product is probably unnecessary. But, you never know *which* fifty percent that is!

TWO
The Appliquéd
Applicant

We must begin somewhere so I'll assume you were born, went to undergraduate school, and that your academic record is pretty much as it will be when you apply to graduate school.

If you still have time to study for your GREs, MATs, or whatever you haven't yet taken, do it! Somehow the mistaken notion has taken hold among undergraduates that it doesn't do any good to study for these types of exams. That notion is wrong, wrong, wrong.

It can and will help you to buy and study one of the several commercial books that are prepared exactly for this purpose. These tests are heavily loaded with informational items. You can discover areas in which your information is scanty by studying one of these commercial *prep books* (see Glossary). You may then read the most elementary college text you can find in these areas to boost your information store. You can even skim such texts and benefit from doing so.

Don't bother with more than one text per area or with advanced texts or books unless you happen to enjoy reading them. The informational items on these tests are at college elementary levels. The single most useful book to study thoroughly is a vocabulary book.

Beyond helping you on informational items, studying a *prep book* will help you understand the rules of the test game before you are actually taking the test. The testing room is no place to suffer the anxiety of realizing that you can interpret the test instructions to mean at least two different things.

In the same vein, a *prep book* on the Graduate Record Exam, for example, can help by forewarning you that questions tend toward requests for "opposite meanings" of words. Supposedly, the idea here is that a synonym merely tests your knowledge of the dictionary meaning of words while an antonym gets at this as well as your "flexibility" (whatever that means) with words.

The very fact that these *prep books* contain items of the sort that are on the actual tests themselves will help you do your best. Practice may not make perfect but it certainly helps to settle the stomach. Whether you have months or only days until you take one of these exams, study a *prep book*. You won't regret it.

If you happen to be in the early part of your junior year when you're reading this (may your tribe increase!), you'll be able to push your test scores up considerably if you'll start now, with a few minutes each day, to prepare for these tests. You can simplify your application campaign, no matter what your grades may be, if you push your test scores up to notable levels.

Even if you've already taken all these tests, there may be time for you to take them again if you're not content with the first set of results. The GREs are given several times a year but you must sign up for them in advance, as you know. Look into it if you think another testing can help.

The graduate departments to which you apply will give most attention to the most recent test results. The faculty who make the admissions decisions believe there are reasons why the first testing might not be the most valid for some people and they are probably correct.

Self-Classification

I'll start by helping you to classify yourself. This *self-classification* (see Glossary) will help you anticipate your prospects for getting in. It will also be of key importance in deciding such things as how many applications to make, what sorts of schools should be considered, and what your chances are for financial aid.

If your anxiety level jumped when I mentioned self-classification you can be sure that this was a completely normal reaction. No one enjoys wondering about "how good" they are unless, of course, something has just happened to indicate that they are "pretty damned good."

But that's not what *this* self-classification is about. There are an uncountable number of ways in which you (and all other human beings) are pretty damned good (or, bad, for that matter). It all depends on which of an uncountable number of standards is used to judge good or bad. This self-classification is about one particular set of standards from among that uncountable number.

There are convincing arguments that this particular set is useless as concerns predicting how a student will do in graduate school and beyond. There are also convincing arguments that this particular set of standards is a valid predictor of future performance. All that is beside the point as far as a realist is concerned. For a realist, the fact is that these standards are used in admission decisions. A realist deals with the world as it is (as far as he can see or discover).

You are, yourself, a part of the world as it is. Where you stand in the self-classification that follows is a part of the world as it is. There is no more benefit in imagining that your standing has some unequivocal meaning about the "essential you" than in wishing the past could be changed. It is what it is. Regret over what might have been won't change anything. Deal with what is. Most people don't, you know. But, they could and so can you. Therefore, read on. Who are you?

Superperson

This book on impression management is not for you unless there is one particular school or program to which you feel you must be accepted if your life is to have any meaning. Your grade-point average (or quality-point ratio, or whatever they call it at your school but to which I will refer as your GPA) is a B+ or A, your GRE scores are 95th percentile or above, and your Miller Analogies Test (MAT) score is 90th percentile or above.

You will also command an enthusiastic letter of recommendation from at least one *big name* (see Glossary) in the academic field in which you majored and are applying. You have certainly assisted one or more names (who were at least *comer names;* see Glossary) in their own research or artistic activities. You may even be a junior co-author of a published article bearing the names of those you assisted with their work.

Unless, as I've said, you feel you must get into a particular program that is known to be difficult to penetrate, your only problem will be in deciding which of several acceptance offers *you* want to take. If you do lust to penetrate a particular program, this book can help you. Otherwise, unless you have a friend to whom you'd like to make a gift, there isn't much you'll gain from buying it. Some, perhaps, but not much. You never really know, do you?

Solidperson

These lessons on impression management can help you. It's true that even without them you may be accepted by a *maximum class* (see Glossary) school.

However, it's worth noting that while the number of doctorates awarded nationally has been slightly downward since 1973, the proportion of doctorates awarded by *maximum class* schools has not declined. This means that there is a better chance for a *solidperson* to get into a *maximum class* school today than there was a few years ago. These schools must be accepting more *solidperson* applicants. That's why the proportion of doctorates they've awarded has not declined, I believe. A well-run application campaign, then, promises to give you more choices among these schools than you might otherwise have had.

Your GPA is B to B+, your GREs are between the 85th and 95th percentiles, and your MAT score is between the 75th and 90th percentiles. You can also count on a letter of recommendation from at least one *comer name* whom you've had the opportunity to either assist or have supervise you in some project.

Maybeperson

There is no question in my mind that this book can help you since it describes ways for you to appear to be a *solidperson* with a history of special difficulties (none of them your fault). This history will assist your gatekeepers to discount the significance of your lower grades, GREs and MAT score.

Your GPA is C+ to B, your GREs are between the 65th and 75th percentiles, and your MAT score is between the 50th and 75th percentiles. You won't be able to count on strong letters of recommendation. You simply haven't come to know any faculty members in your undergraduate department all that well. Don't despair if this is the case. I will tell you later how to finesse any faculty member into writing a good letter for you when I discuss stalking references.

Gambleperson

This book is most likely to help you if at least one of the parts of your *hard credentials* is much better than the other parts.

For example, suppose your GPA is a flat C, your MAT score is at the 40th percentile, your GRE Verbal and GRE Advanced scores around the 45th percentile, *but* your GRE Quantitative score is at the 85th percentile (see Glossary for definitions of these subscores). The distinctly higher score on this one part of the GRE can be the means by which you help your gatekeepers to discount the significance of all of the rest of your *hard credentials*.

By the way, in case you've forgotten or never been told, a score at a given percen*tile* is one below which the indicated percen*tage* of a comparison group has scored. The same raw test score may be at very different percentiles depending upon which comparison group is used as a standard. So, your MAT score might put you at the 75th percentile compared to theology majors but at the 25th percentile compared to physics majors. This isn't a slur on theology majors. It just reflects the fact that more physics majors scored at your level on the MAT than did theology majors. You will receive a raw score. The MAT Prep Book published by Baron's Educational Service, Inc., will give you an idea of the percentile equivalents of various raw scores. I apologize for this minilecture but, remember, I'm an academician, too. It's hard to fight the characteristic urge to constantly explain things to people—whether or not they've asked.

To return, then, to the *gambleperson* with a notably high GRE Quantitative score surrounded by middling scores everywhere else. In some fields (psychology being one), a high quantitative score has a fatal attraction to gatekeepers. Perhaps this is because in these fields all academicians can talk, but few can calculate without the aid of a fearfully expensive computer. Such persons can be led to develop a very positive attitude toward a student who *can* calculate if such an activity is at all common in the given field. Statistical analysis is common in a wide variety of social sciences, and even in some of the humanities. A *gambleperson* who shows promise of being capable of learning to use such analyses can capitalize on this strength while letting his weaknesses simply fade from sight.

Which (happily) unusual part of the *hard credentials* can be emphasized with profit will differ from one group of academic fields to another. Obviously, if you were planning to apply in English, the pattern I've described will not be particularly attractive to your gatekeepers. Even so, all is not lost.

I wrote earlier that I'd try to help you think *creatively* about the system. Let me ask, then, what might a *gambleperson* who was planning on graduate studies in English do, given this set of *hard credentials?*

If you answered, "Plow ahead in English and trust to luck," you haven't got your mind right yet. If you answered, "Find out what other graduate major field there is in which this set of *hard credentials* might be more attractive," you have hit it right on the button.

Sound odd? Do I mean you should actually change your field because of the numbers on various parts of your *hard credentials?* Not necessarily, although it might turn out that way (at your choice, of course).

First, let's remember I'm discussing the circumstances of a *gambleperson.* A realist deals with the world as it is.

Second, once you've decided to go to graduate school the highest priority is to get in.

Third, once you're in graduate school it's usually easier to transfer into another given program than it was to be accepted to it in the first place. For one thing, you're on the scene and can make personal contacts with the gatekeepers in your *target department* (see Glossary). For another, once you've taken some graduate courses in something, your performance there will command inordinate weight among the *hard credentials* you present for transfer.

I think of this plan as the *area shift* (see Glossary). It is closely related to the *stepping stones to anywhere* (see Glossary) plan that I will describe later. The *area shift* moves you from program to program within a given university while *stepping stones* moves you from university to university within a given program. Both are useable by people of any classification but the *gambleperson* may have more need for one or the other.

Yourekiddingperson

It would be false if I told you I really believed that this book will help you get in. Still, my opinion could be wrong about that since there are, as I've said, a staggering number of graduate programs needing students each year.

This doesn't mean that I haven't, myself, seen applications bearing D to C − GPAs and GREs in the range of the 5th to the 35th percentile over three testing sessions. I have.

A particular *yourekiddingperson* may have had such a

run of bad luck, oppressive life circumstances, and other difficulties that an entirely invalid picture is presented by his *hard credentials.* Only that individual is in a position to judge whether he really wants to go to graduate school so much, and is willing to work so hard, that if he can just get one shot the picture will change completely.

If you think you're that person, *now* is the time to be very realistic about how much you do want it and how hard you're ready to work. While you're thinking it over, don't neglect to consider that there are many satisfying ways to live a life without going to graduate school. Remember, too, that those in skilled trades or business will undoubtedly earn more money in a lifetime than I will ever approach in mine.

Guesstimating

Depending on when you're reading this book you may or may not have all of the details of your *hard credentials* in hand and I hope you haven't yet collected or prepared your *soft credentials.* If you haven't you should guesstimate how they'll appear with the cold eye of a realist inspecting a used car. This is no time to kid yourself.

Your GPA through February of your last undergraduate year is the only GPA your gatekeepers will see so fix on that one. Also, calculate your GPA for your last two years as well as your GPA in your major courses. Many gatekeepers are most interested in these last two GPAs because your overall GPA probably includes a number of courses that are "guts" or "mickey mouses" or "snaps." You should miss no opportunity to call attention to the *highest* of these three GPAs, however.

Both the Miller Analogies Test and the Graduate Record Examination are given by appointment at designated testing centers. However, the testing dates that can be arranged for the MAT are almost always more frequent during the year than the dates set for the GRE.

If you can arrange to take the MAT early in your application campaign, you can use the score you receive to estimate your likely GRE Verbal score. The formula for doing this is GREV = 216 + 6(MAT). This equation provides only a *rough* estimate and doesn't work very well for MAT scores above 90. However, if your MAT raw score is above 90 on this 100-item test, just congratulate yourself and don't bother about conversions.

If it happens that you've already taken the GRE, then the equivalent conversion formula to estimate your likely MAT score is MAT = (GREV/6) - 36. That is, just divide your GREV score by six and then subtract 36 to get your estimated MAT score.

You can also estimate your probable GRE percentile ranking on the GRE Verbal and GRE Quantitative subtests by taking the practice tests in the prep book published by the Arco Publishing Company on the GRE. You must take these practice tests under the exact conditions specified by the directions. If you don't follow the practice test directions, you'll only be kidding yourself. This prep book contains an unofficial percentile ranking table for your scores on the practice tests that estimates what your percentile ranking would be on the GRE test itself.

Your judgment about your probable soft credentials should not be hard and fast at this stage. A good part of this book is devoted to telling you how to acquire soft credentials that will put you in the most attractive light.

Still, even at an early stage of your application campaign you'll have some idea of your prospects for contacting *big names, comer names,* and *big frogs* (see Glossary).

For one thing, you'll know if you have or haven't had personal contact with some faculty member already. You may not know his name status but you'll know whether you're starting from scratch or not. I'll tell you later how to discover his name status but your campaign will be less time consuming if you have already had some sort of personal contact.

For another thing, you'll have some idea whether the faculty at your undergraduate school do research. If it's a university, you can be sure they do (or have at some time) or they'd never have been awarded tenure. Anyone who's been around for more than six years almost surely has tenure at any university. If they're newcomers and young, you can be sure they are either doing research or they won't be there for long.

If you're at a college, the faculty may or may not do research depending on the "orientation" of the school. At some, research is necessary for academic survival and at others it may even be thought to interfere with effective teaching.

In general, you'll have better prospects for effective letters of recommendation if your home school faculty are doing or have done a lot of research. It is through their research publications, primarily, that they become known to the gatekeepers at the universities to which you'll apply for graduate study. It is through their research publications, primarily, that they have or will acquire name status. It follows that there is more potential for acquiring strong soft credentials if you are where research is happening.

Another Encouraging Word

As you guesstimate your hard credentials and potential for good soft credentials, compare them with the self-classification categories I've described.

You may find that you don't fit cleanly into one category but span the boundaries of two neighboring categories. A *boundary spanner* (see Glossary) is in need of a managed impression since, otherwise, the message conveyed will be complex. Complex messages confuse gatekeepers (Principle 4).

Even if you span the boundaries of three categories you may still not have an unmanageable campaign ahead of you. If your hard credentials are strongish but you can't for the life of you imagine any faculty member even recognizing you — don't worry. I'll fix that. If your hard credentials are weakish but you know a *big name* as you would a father — again, don't worry. That is even easier to fix.

But do try to hone down your self-classification in the most realistic way you can. How many applications you should make and where you should make them will depend on your having a good view of yourself in terms of the admissions standards used by graduate schools.

Getting Started

The first mistake you will be tempted to make is to go to your academic advisor for advice. However reasonable that may seem to you, do *not* do it. At least don't do it yet!

The first thing to consider is that there are advisors and then there are *advisors*. You may have known only one or two individuals called academic advisors but I have known and talked to a lot of them.

Some advisors are actively on your side. I hope you've had one of this kind. It is safe to talk with this kind of advisor about many things you should never dream of mentioning to the other kind.

Still, there are some things better not shared with even a truly supportive advisor. It may make it easier for him to write a letter of recommendation if he truly thinks that what he knows about you is all there is to know.

Of course, if your helpful advisor recommends this book to you, there's no point treading carefully because that means *he's* a realist. A realistic advisor is a pearl beyond price and you may safely pump him about anything that crosses your mind concerning graduate school.

You can recognize the other kind of advisor by the brevity of his past conversations with you. All he wanted to do was sign whatever papers you needed signed and get you out of his office.

Whatever type of advisor you may have, you can be sure of one thing. He will expect to be asked to write a letter of recommendation for you if you apply to graduate school. So, unless he's a realist, you should be careful never to suggest that you don't know exactly what you're doing. Recall Principle 3; you should defend your image, even with your very own advisor.

Almost all departments in which graduate education is available are staffed by faculty who are members of some national professional association. In psychology, for example, this national group is the American Psychological Association, and each of the traditional academic disciplines will have its own version of this national organization. Your reference librarian will be able to identify this organization in the area *or areas* (remember the *area shift* I mentioned as a possibility for the gambleperson?) of interest to you. The first person you should consult is the reference librarian in your school library—even if you have a realistic advisor. The librarian can also direct you to library holdings of the *house journal* (see Glossary) of the relevant national group. This will be a gold mine of the sorts of information useful in the beginnings of your collection of inside information (Principle 2).

At this stage of getting started, you may be toying with two or three possible areas of graduate study (e.g., credential considerations might warrant thinking about sociology, anthropology, or even philosophy for graduate work). You may, of course, have settled on one area. Whichever it is, a reading of a few issues in the most recent year of the *house journal* of the field of interest should be your next step.

You should not concentrate on so-called substantive articles in the *house journal*. These might have such titles as "A Reappraisal of Wilhelm Wundt" or "Interpersonal Dynamics in a Simulated Prison: A Methodological Analysis." Such articles actually concern the content of field, and that is not your primary concern at the moment.

What you should look for (and read) are articles with titles such as "Placement Report: 1973 and 1974." One such titled article in the *American Psychologist* concerned the percentage distribution of positions offered degreed psychologists by private industry, academic institutions, hospitals, and the federal government in those years at the annual convention placement service — or *meat market* as it is known in the trade. Another such useful article might be "An Overview of Psychology's Human Resources: Characteristics and Salaries from the 1972 APA Survey" — a gem for the purposes of the potential psychology graduate student, concerning demographic characteristics of about thirty-five thousand psychologists, percentage distributions of sub-area specializations, salaries, work activities, and types of degrees.

You should also ask the librarian to lead you to the annual publication of the National Research Council. The one I have before me is titled *Summary Report 1977: Doctorate Recipients from United States Universities*. No matter when you're reading this book, there'll be one for the most recent year and you'll find it extremely informative. It almost certainly won't matter what speciality you're in, either. Your field will be included in this summary of trends in numbers of doctoral awards in each field, what class of institutions granted how many Ph.D.'s, and other useful goodies.

This information will be helpful to you in estimating the probable *entrance competitiveness* in various specialities as well as whether the number of Ph.D.'s has dropped so much that *four years from your entrance* there will be an insufficient supply in a given field.

On the matter of supply, the regular cycle is that the employment market becomes glutted by an oversupply in a field, enrollments begin to decline, the number of Ph.D.'s necessarily declines, and a few years later employers are eager to recruit the diminished number of new Ph.D.'s that are then trickling out of graduate schools. Eventually, that word gets around to undergraduates and enrollments begin to shift back into the now undersupplied specialty.

For most graduate students it's a matter of sheer good luck if they happen to hit the job market when there's an undersupply. I'm suggesting here that you look ahead as best you can to what the employment market will be four years from the time you start graduate school. It's close to suggesting you try to read tea leaves, I know, but a realist does the best he can with what's available.

So, now is the time to consider such matters — now, before you make even the miniscule commitment entailed in applying to graduate school in sociology, rather than anthropology, or psychology, or whatever. Let your fellow undergraduates decide what they're going to be on the basis of a starry-eyed delusion that what the world needs is more social workers, engineers, physicists, agronomists, or psychologists. *You* decide on the only realistic basis that an individual member of any species has ever successfully used: how can I survive? Please note, I am not saying you need be uncivilized about such survival-oriented behavior or ignore your own substantive interests. Just take the system for what it really is and seek to have the choices you make now cause you minimum grief later.

Where, Oh Where?

Having now done some exploring for useful information about one or more prospective kingdoms, you (along with every other undergraduate I've ever known) face two questions. The first is, "Where should I apply?" The second is, "How many applications should I make?"

As to the questions of where, you may think this is familiar ground that you've trod when applying for undergraduate school. To the contrary, I think this earlier experience has contaminated your mind as concerns applying to graduate school. Ever the realist, I will tell you a plain fact: The graduate schools to which you apply should not be chosen on the basis of local climate, ratio of male to female registrants, or the availability of first-run movies in the immediate vicinity.

There are only two factors of primary importance and one factor of secondary importance in deciding on which graduate schools you should consider.

The number one factor is the likelihood that you can get in. The number two factor is the *class* of the particular department within the field in which you plan to study. The distant third factor is the compatibility of what you think to be your present interests with the program that will admit you. That's all there are; there are no more. You may not believe me and I will not try to cajole you into believing me. I will, however, tell you my reasons for what I've said.

The importance of the first factor (to any but a *superperson* and I doubt that many such are still with me) should be obvious. If you can't get in, nothing else is relevant.

The importance of the second factor is due to existing academic practices in hiring newly degreed people as faculty members (having such a job one day is, after all, one of the reasons you may be going through this hassle now). What I mean is this: if there is any possible way (however marginally legal it may be in these days of Affirmative Action), departments hire new people trained in other departments of equal or higher class than the hiring department. Only under rare circumstances does someone trained at Unknown U have a chance to be hired by Super U. At the same time, a Super U graduate has a good shot at all the other *maximum class* places and everything on down to Unknown U. But, notice, the same pecking order in hiring selection operates at all class levels. If you get in to a *middle class* graduate department, you'll have a good shot at being hired by other *middle class* departments, an excellent chance at *lower class* departments, and a near cinch at *no class* departments (see Glossary).

It has been the subject of occasional speculation that the class of a department has something to do with the quality of the faculty but that is beside the point here. Within rather broad limits I personally doubt that this speculation is true, anyway. The point you should consider is where you can do the best you can, given your credentials and impression potential, because the better you do now, the more job options will be available to you when you finish your degree work. I will have more to say later about how truly simple it is to estimate the class level of departments of graduate study in which you may be interested.

This may sound as if I'm saying that a person who doesn't get into a *maximum class* department is slated for a life of second-rate everything. Nothing could be further from my meaning or intentions.

The reality is that your best chance at a *first* job is in an institution of the same or lower class as your graduate university. There are exceptions, of course, but that's still a plain fact in the general case.

But, there are two other realities as well. First, there are scads of places other than *maximum class* universities where things are very much first rate. Second, just as the *stepping stones to anywhere* plan can move a graduate student from the local junior college to Super U through successive transfers, so can this same plan move a faculty member through successive jobs. All it takes is research work, publications, and a willingness to move a mess of times.

It may have puzzled you when I wrote that the compatibility of your present interests with the program that will admit you is only a distant third factor in deciding where to apply. If you weren't puzzled, you are really beginning to think creatively and I congratulate you.

Even if you have narrowed your target to a single academic field, I have two reasons for advising you to keep this factor in proper (i.e., if only distant) perspective. The first is that except in the most haphazard terms you really cannot judge such compatibility. The second is that you have absolutely no idea of how much your interests will change when you actually begin to find out something about the field after you're in graduate school. Why, then, ask I the realist, should you let fanciful ideas about such unassessable and possibly transient compatibility restrict your options?

What? You say you've wanted to be a marine ichthyologist since you were given a gold fish at the age of four? So what? If you can't get into a department for such training, why not apply to one in some allied field? You'll still have a number of options. You might find a way to wiggle, squirm, or otherwise insert your body into marine ichthyology after you've arrived to study in the allied field. Or, you might discover that the allied field has an absolutely fascinating speciality area in the dentistry of deep sea fishes. Don't restrict yourself because the attainable departments of lower class in one field have blinded you to closely related departments of higher class.

Exactly the same realistic logic applies to those of you who have decided that you are going to be an astronomer, chemist, mathematician, psychologist, zoologist, or whatever one training speciality is fixed in your sights.

If you must go into psychology (to take a speciality with which I'm intimately familiar), for heaven's sake don't lose sight of the fact that there are many rooms in this particular house. One is called clinical psychology (I'd bet you know about that one if you've ever even heard of psychology; most people who apply for graduate training in psychology hope to study clinical psychology). One is called experimental psychology (such arrogance; you'd think we social psychologists never did an experiment). One is called child psychology (at really *in* places this one may be called developmental psychology but don't let that fool you, it's still child psychology). And last, but not least (comes the revolution, that is), is one called social psychology. The point of this roll call being, of course, that if you must be a psychologist, and are less than a *superperson*, why apply for a sub-area in psychology (i.e., clinical psychology) that is distinguished mainly by the enormous numbers of *superpersons* applying for it? Impression management is one thing—a miracle is quite another.

Do you see what I'm driving at? Just as psychology is divided into rooms, so too is every other academic speciality that has been in existence for more than ten years (this

period apparently being necessary for its pioneering
founders to overcome their astonishment that anyone is
taking them seriously, to establish one or more journals in
this new area, and to begin arguing with one another).
And, among sub-areas within a given field, there will be
differences in (a) the numbers of persons who apply to
them, (b) the mix of persons who apply to them, and (c)
the amount of elbow room that exists for you to manage
your impression.

If you simply won't be satisfied unless you are a plasma
physicist and that happens to be the hottest current sub-
area in physics, why not apply in something a little cooler
in which you won't have to buck every *superperson* who
happens also to want to be a plasma physicist?

Get into physics in the highest class department you can
manage and then worry about arranging a *sub-area shift*
(see Glossary) into plasma physics if you can. If you can't?
Who knows, you may come to love what you have. And,
even if you don't come to love it, you may still take a
master's degree in it and on the basis of that one year or
two of graduate work (which unduly impresses admissions
committees, in my experience, but that is far from your
problem) apply for more advanced work at another
department in plasma physics. Creative? I think so. In
fact, this is the *stepping stones to anywhere* plan I mentioned earlier and, believe me, it has and will continue to
work just fine.

I have stated my advice on this point rather vehemently.
At the same time, I don't want to leave you with the idea
that deciding where (and in what) to apply for graduate
study should bear no relation whatsoever to your present
interests. It *is* a factor (a distant third, as I put it earlier).
My reasons for making so much noise about having an
open mind on this matter are based on my own experiences

with my advisees. To be blunt, the chances are very, very great that you have not considered that there was any question about the primary importance of compatibility between your interests and where you apply. You may not have had any idea what you wanted to be as you started undergraduate school but if you have reached the point of deciding to go to graduate school, you are now convinced that you know what you want to be.

I take to be one of the things of value I have to offer you in this book the repeated exhortation to think big, to think creatively, and not take anything for granted. If I succeed in getting you to think about matters that have never occurred to you—even if you then decide to proceed as you initially intended—I will at least have given you the chance to make that decision with your eyes wide open. Nothing is forever, except death; you can always change your mind. But it costs a little more sometimes.

Having done my best to get your mind right on the factors which should determine where to apply, I'll turn to the question of how you may estimate the class of a department in your field (i.e., physics, philosophy, or zoology).

The first standard you should apply (particularly for screening purposes when you are initially working up a manageable list for further consideration) is utterly simple. Academicians accept the same kinds of status claims that have sold products to Americans for years: Big Is Better, Most Expensive Is Best.

They would, of course, deny it. They would observe that quantity does not imply quality. They might even chuckle if you suggested they accept such a silly *falsism*. I assure you, however, that you can depend on the fact that in their eyes the biggest departments in their field in the biggest universities in the land are the *maximum class* departments.

I've said this standard is utterly simple. In saying that, I smoothed over the companion qualification that age of the university acts as a multiplier in determining the class of departments within given fields. If you choose, you may ignore the age multiplier since sheer physical largeness in faculty, facilities, and federal grants is, by itself, the most powerful determinant of a department's class in the pecking order of the field.

Keep always in mind the truth that class level is *someone's* subjective assessment for there is no way of measuring objectively that which is fundamentally an attribute of value. It is, therefore, your task to estimate which departments are believed by the gatekeepers you will face (persons writing reference letters, admisssions committee members, search committee members who are seeking to hire newly degreed faculty . . .) to be *maximum, middle, lower* and *no class* departments.

In fact, you would be well advised to remind yourself regularly that the class of a department may have little to do with its quality. When I write of classes, I'm merely using this label to designate an attribute that exists in the minds of academicians. I don't, myself, let such labels camouflage the fact that competence is where you find it, whether in *maximum* or *no class* departments. The same is true of incompetence.

How can you begin to decide on a listing of this sort? One useful rule-of-thumb is this: Ignore anything in the South, except North Carolina and Texas; include the entire West Coast, East and Northeast; include any state university in the Central United States. Do not even think about states in the immediate vicinity of Wyoming unless you are planning to apply in certain of the biological sciences (some very classy departments concerned with wild life studies are to be found in this Northern Rocky Mountain area). This is a rough rule so don't feel you are bound by it if you happen upon conflicting information.

With these areas in mind, then, you'll turn to a source of more specific information. I will cite it for you here.

This reference (or, as you should come to think of it, your *playbook*) is: *A Rating of Graduate Programs* by Kenneth D. Roose and Charles J. Anderson; it was published by the American Council on Education [ACE] 1785 Massachusetts Ave., N.W., Washington, D.C. 20036 in 1970. Check with your friend the reference librarian. Such people are very good at their work and they love finding things for you.

This *playbook* contains the results of an opinion survey among 6,093 academicians. The sample consisted of department chairmen (21 percent of the sample), senior scholars (41 percent of the sample), and junior scholars (38 percent of the sample). All were asked to rate departments in their own field in 130 universities on such things as Quality of Graduate Faculty, Effectiveness of the Doctoral Program, and Change in the Last five Years. If your mouth is not watering at the prospect of reading all the resulting inside information this *playbook* contains, you really haven't appreciated the meaning of Principle 2.

If you are troubled by the fact that this survey was conducted in 1969 and you are reading this book in 1984, don't be. If there is anything that is difficult to change, it is an academician's opinion (on any subject). It is my belief that the judgments contained in this *playbook* are sufficiently stable for your purposes so that you may be safely guided by them until somewhere around the year 2000. If you don't trust my belief on this, you might check an earlier study of the same sort (this one conducted in 1964) which was also published by the ACE. That reference is: *An Assessment of Qualilty in Graduate Education* and is known as the Cartter (Allan M.) survey in the more recent *playbook*. Other than a little minor shifting, the *maximum class* is still the *maximum class* and so on down the line.

While I'll draw on bits of information contained in this playbook that you need in deciding on where to apply (as well as the closely coupled matter of the likelihood you'll get in), at the moment I'll mention only one of its features. The raters were asked to judge, let us say, Quality of Graduate Faculty in the departments in their field in each of the listed universities according to the categories Distinguished, Strong (both *maximum class* in my terminology), Good *(middle class* in my words), Adequate *(lower class)*, and Not Sufficient for Doctoral Training *(no class* in my lexicon).

They were also permitted to state they had Insufficient Information to make judgment. However, apparently from a delicate concern for the feelings of members of *no class* departments, the report itself does not openly list which departments received the fateful rating Not Sufficient for Doctoral Training.

Any realist could look more deeply into which of these departments were probably judged Not Sufficient by comparing the list of institutions included in the survey with the institutions' rankings in a given specialty area. If Allamagoosa University was one of the institutions included in the survey but not one listed with even an Adequate Plus (i.e., *lower class*) rating in, say, mathematics, it's probably a *no class* place in fancy figuring. It could be that none of the raters thought they had sufficient information to judge Allamagoosa but I wouldn't bet my own money on it.

Still, this would be particularly valuable information for the *gambleperson* since the odds are good that the competition for entrance to Allamagoosa in mathematics will be low. And, even they must take in new graduate students to keep the shop in operation.

To be complete about it, there's the third possibility that Allamagoosa grants a master's degree only in mathematics but was included because it grants Ph.D.'s in other specialities. In an old-line field such as mathematics that's not too likely but it could be the case here and there.

Such *M.A. only farm clubs* (see Glossary) are not to be ignored wherever they are found. This is especially true for *maybepersons* and *gamblepersons*. These programs are often the keys to initiating the *stepping stones to anywhere* plan I mentioned earlier.

This plan involves getting into an *M.A. only* department, taking graduate work for about a year and then transferring on the basis of that record to a somewhat higher class school. You needn't even complete a master's degree at your first school — or at your second, or third, or at however many you are personally willing to move through on your way to the class of school you plan to reach for your Ph.D. degree study.

While this sort of bootstrapping may extend your period of graduate study for a few years, you may think the investment is worth it if you really want to get into a school that would not have glanced at your credentials had you applied directly from undergraduate school.

The thing you must do now is to begin shaping your *preliminary list* (see Glossary) of schools where you may apply. Your *playbook* will be used in this shaping, but you'll also need another reference. This one will tell you what fields of study exist (and whether they grant an M.A., a Ph.D., or both) at all the universities and colleges in the United States (well, almost all; I doubt that anyone even has a list of all of them). Think of this next one as your *program*.

This source is excellent because it's updated annually. Its title is *The Annual Guides to Graduate Study* (Peterson's Guides, Inc., Princeton, N.J.). There are eight volumes in

my own set of Peterson's (as everyone calls this directory).
I've no idea how many there may be by the time you read
this but that doesn't mean you must plow through all of
these volumes.

Book I contains general descriptions of individual
graduate institutions. Also, it is a "locator" volume for
sub-area descriptions of much greater detail to be found in
one of the remaining Books. My set contains the following
academic areas:

Book   III Biological and Health Sciences
Book   IV   Administrative, Environmental, and Social
             Sciences
Book   V   Arts, Letters, and Communication
Book   VI   Education and Nursing
Book   VII Engineering and Applied Sciences
Book   VIII Physical Sciences

You will need to consult only Book I and one of the
other volumes. Try your library first; each volume sells for
about seven dollars if you decide to buy your own. You
may not even be free to decide since one or two other
students may have heard of Peterson's, thus making it hard
to find in the library when you need it.

Locate the pages that apply to your target departments.
You can then refer to them when it comes time to write
your statement of interests and career plans (see chapter
five, Your Heart's Desire).

Your Peterson's will, as a good *program* should, tell you
in which sub-areas each and every university offers graduate degrees of what kind, as well as what each department
has to say about itself. Don't believe everything you read
but do read it. It would be a good idea to check the other
possible sources listed in the back of this volume (An
Obscure Appendix) as you narrow down your choices.

Some sources will contain information not contained in the others although there's a great deal of overlap.

Using your *playbook* and *program*, adopt the following rule-of-thumb in deciding on about four schools (I should really say departments since a creative person may be reserving decision about exactly which fields are to be targeted and will need as many *preliminary lists* as fields in hand) in each of the class levels recommended. If you are a *solidperson* who can sell himself as a *superperson* (I ignore real *superpersons*; they only need help getting into a *particular* school), you'll want schools in the *maximum* and *middle class*. If you are a *maybeperson* you'll want schools in the *middle* and *lower class*. If you are a *gambleperson*, you will seek schools in the middle, lower, and no class categories (always remembering that some of those no class schools will be *M.A. only farm clubs*, and as I've implied, these are not necessarily without class in the view of those schools granting Ph.D.'s which regularly collect a harvest from them).

Now perhaps you've begun to see why I went through the process of helping you with a self-classification. The two primary factors in deciding where to apply are (1) the likelihood that you'll get in, and (2) class of the departments to which you should direct your applications. A realistic self-classification is the key to blending these two factors together to permit the beginnings of a shaped selection process in which you aim at the most likely targets.

How Many, Oh Lord?

The number of applications you should make (as well as the mix of applications to likely classes of departments) depends on a number of factors. First among these is, again, your person classification. You may have noticed that the *gambleperson* was advised to identify four schools in each of only two classes. It is sad but true that even in the impression management game, them that hasn't must work a little harder than them that has.

Your estimation of the level of competiveness for entrance into the field(s) you've chosen is another major factor in deciding on the number of applications you'll make. You may be sure that *superpersons* and *solidpersons* tend to be more concentrated among applicants to the hottest areas of the moment. The publication I'll cite in the last section of this chapter (GPAM) will provide you enrollment information to use in estimating entrance competitiveness.

The third major factor is your realistic estimate of your own energy reserve (i.e., stamina, grit, determination). I'll hint at why energy reserve is important here by forewarning you that each application you'll prepare, if you follow my advice in detail, will be uniquely created to fit the needs of the particular gatekeepers at each graduate school to which you apply. There'll be no writing one draft of your statement of interests and career plans with copies to all schools to which you apply; that would be wasting your finest opportunity to be the unique person that each gatekeeper needs. You may not yet realize how much work is involved in filling out all those forms that each school will send you. That amount of work is child's play by comparison with what following all my advice will entail. Of course, you may decide to take only some of my advice and that's all right, too. Even then you'll be miles ahead of the ordinary applicant.

Simply because your *preliminary list* contains four schools in each of the recommended classes does not mean that you'll make eight (or twelve) applications. You might think about doing that to be completely safe. But, again I counsel realism. Channel your undoubtedly growing anxiety about what will happen if no one takes you into more productive activities than mere multiplication of the number of applications you make. Save your energy. You'll need it.

Solidpersons who can appear as (in some ways) *superpersons* should plan on at least three applications to *maximum class* departments and at least two applications to *middle class* departments. These numbers are not, by the way, simply made up out of my head. They are partly based on my experience with my own undergraduate advisees in past years and partly on published data which I have examined.

Since it is very unlikely that I would be permitted by the copyright holders of the journals in which these data have appeared to reprint their tables (my guess is that they would be stuffy about what some would call my irreverent attitude), I have not troubled to ask for such releases. I can, however, cite one such source and urge you to search for such data in the *house journal* of your field.

An example of the sort of thing I refer to is: "The 1967 Graduate Applicant Cohort in Psychology" by J. Cates (*American Psychologist*, 1972, *27*, 453-56). This fascinating article presents some of the data from a survey of the 18,385 applicants to some graduate program (that bunch of people is called a cohort in *clubspeak*; see Glossary) in psychology for the 1967-1968 academic year. This particular article, for example, records that of those making three applications, 56.5 percent were accepted somewhere and of those making two applications, 51.8 percent were accepted somewhere—and that cohort consisted (in my opinion) of people who mostly paid as little attention to artful impression management as the many, many applications I've seen personally. And, I would guess, many were *superpersons*, too.

If a *solidperson* doesn't have better than a 50 percent chance by following my advice I have been living on Mars all these years! And, please note, I am advising five applications in all from such a person. The percentage accepted somewhere of those making five applications was, according to Cates, 68.8 percent.

Of course, I hasten to qualify that somewhere isn't necessarily a *maximum* or *middle class* department and if you, as an actual *solidperson*, just can't stand the fearful strain of worrying that no one will take you from those two classes, hedge, if you must. Apply to one *lower class* department. This *insurance school* (see Glossary) will be delighted. The only concern you might have here is that you will look so good to them that they'll be convinced that you will never accept an offer of admission. They might not, therefore, want to tie up a financial aid offer with you that would then be unavailable to entice their typical applicant. I'll have more to say about how you can avoid being treated as a *nochance applicant* (see Glossary) at an insurance school as concerns financial aid stipends.

Before I move on, I should mention to those *yourekiddingpersons* who are still reading and thinking about graduate school, Cates reports that of those making ten or more applications only 75.5 percent were accepted somewhere. Graduate schools *everywhere* do turn down *some* applicants.

If you are a *maybeperson*, you, too, should make five applications in all. Three will be to *middle class* and two to *lower class* departments; and, yes, there is no way I can stop you from applying to one *insurance school* of *lower class* if you simply cannot manage your anxiety. At least, if you do make an application to an *insurance school*, try to make it one that is an *M.A. only farm club* in as big a state university as possible. Assuming you go there you will, of course, have to transfer elsewhere at the end of a year or two (e.g., *stepping stones to anywhere* plan) after receipt of a master's degree but the sheer size of the university will insure that the departments to which you'll apply will have heard of your erstwhile school. That counts; I meant it when I said that academicians believe that *bigger is better*. Americans believe it; why shouldn't American academicians?

If you are a *gambleperson*, you should make more applications even though you are working on a *maybeperson* paint job. I recommend one to the *middle class* (and this may well prove to be an arrow shot into nowhere but I've known of some wild shots that did bring down fat ducks), three to the *lower class* departments on your list, and three to the *no class* places you've tentatively targeted.

It is especially important that you have *M.A. only farm clubs* on your *no class* list. As I said earlier, these are not necessarily without class and these *M.A. only* programs are often totally overlooked by applicants. They are still there, they still have faculty that must justify their continuing existence, they must have graduate student bodies. Offer them yours.

I've advised you to collect a *preliminary list* of from eight to twelve schools. However, at most, the number of applications any person should make is seven (*gambleperson*) and the least is five applications (*solidperson*). But, even at $15 per nonrefundable fee, that comes to between $75 and $105 for those numbers of applications. And, presumably, all but $15 of it will do you no good whatever. That is not to be tolerated unless you happen to be well fixed financially.

What to do about it? Just include a separate typed and signed letter with each application in which you state that it is too great a financial burden for you to pay the fee. Ask that the fee be waived in your case for this reason.

I've seen such letters from creative realists and the result was the fee was simply waived. Perhaps that's because so few people request a waiver that it's easier to grant a few than worry about it. And, please notice, the worst that might happen if you make this request is that some clerk in the graduate school will send you a canned letter in which you are told that policy prevents waiver without some special procedure. If that happens, just send the fifteen bucks and let it go at that.

Since I'm assuming that you're not all that able to lay out such fee money without feeling burdened, your request for a waiver is the truth. And, if only one school waives the fee (though more will probably do it), you've more than paid for this book.

As far as I'm concerned this application fee is just one more tax on people whose education is, itself, a future benefit to society. That's not my brand of gin and I say to hell with it (to quote W. C. Fields).

And now, what about those schools on your list to which you'll not apply eventually? Why those? Well, for one thing, some of the information I'll soon be advising you to collect may steer you more toward one or two schools in a given class rather than others in that same class on your *preliminary list*. That is, again, it's a matter of keeping some options open even though you're now starting to settle on a limited number of schools for further investigation.

For another thing, some of the good advice you'll get from your academic advisor may lead you to think more seriously about one rather than another school on your list. And, it won't hurt the impression you make with him if there is every sign that you are taking his good advice. Your chances of having a school on your list that you've already investigated and he knows something about are greater with more schools listed.

Last, and this will make more sense to you when you read the chapter on letters of recommendation, you should try to include on your *preliminary list* the schools from which your probable references received their own graduate degrees. This might even mean including a school not in one of the classes or one of the locales recommended; if so, you'll need a slightly larger list than eight to twelve schools. There are many simple ways to determine any faculty member's graduate alma mater. I'll mention some later but, for now, test your own creativity by thinking how you'd do it, without asking, of course. There is a good reason for this that I'll tell you about later.

Pinpointing the Nitty Gritty

As soon as you have your *preliminary list*, write for all applications, information, and anything having to do with financial aid. Your *program* will provide the mailing addresses you'll need. Most schools have a standard package of stuff they'll send. You will not actually use these materials from all of the schools on your *preliminary list* but start them coming through the mails. A stamp is cheap and time will soon be precious.

I've already referred to the existence of national professional organizations given to the care and cultivation of individual academic fields. As I said, the American Psychological Association is the group devoted to the business of psychology, and it publishes an annual guide to graduate programs that is heavily loaded with financial aid information. Your field will have its equivalent association and this group cares very much about the location and funding of its own graduate programs.

You can find the title of the guide in your field (along with name and address of your national association) in one of the four volumes of *Graduate Programs and Admissions Manual* (GPAM) published annually by the Educational Testing Service. Each volume is devoted to one cluster of academic fields and contains a wealth of sub-area information. You'll need only the volume in which your field is to be found.

The four volumes are : A. Agriculture and forestry, the biological sciences, and the health sciences; B. The fine and applied arts, architecture, the classics, philosophy, religion, and languages; C. The physical sciences, mathematics and computer sciences, and engineering; D. The social sciences and education.

In a pinch, you can use the GPAM as your *program* even though it does not contain quite as much information as Peterson's. For present purposes, check the bibliography in GPAM. It will list the most current guide to graduate programs published by the national association in your field. Then go talk to your reference librarian before spending your own money on the guide you've located.

You should plan to have received the necessary application materials early in your seventh semester. This is particularly important for financial aid applications. The deadlines for these are sometimes much earlier than those for application to graduate school itself. Several schools have financial aid deadlines as early as February 1 and it is virtually certain that the decision-making process has begun before the deadline. As a general rule, never trust that a "closing date" is the real deadline. Apply for everything early. It won't hurt and it could make all the difference there is.

I'll have much more to say about financial aid in the last chapter. For now, take it from me that you have a lot to do before January of your senior year. You can do it; thousands have. You can do it well; hundreds have.

And, you'll have an edge. You'll have advice from a realist who has been there.

THREE
The Filleted
Application

The ultimate application package you'll assemble is a thing of many splendors. These (as Gaul) may be divided into three parts.

First, there is that part in which you will say things about yourself. Second, there is that part in which others will say things about you. And, last, there is that part in which you have said things about yourself in course grades earned, GREs, and MATs.

The first part consists of a basic application form, a financial aid application, and statement in which you are asked to describe your academic activities and goals.

On Hard and Soft Parts

I'll postpone discussing the financial aid form for now so let's turn to other hard and soft sections in this first part. Typical of the hard information here are such things as your name, address, and undergraduate college. Hard information is that which you are morally or practically help-

57

less to shape in ways which are more fitting to the image
you want to project.

It is notable (to one reared in my generation in which all
indications of ethnicity on applications were officially and
legally proscribed lest discrimination creep into decisions)
that most graduate schools today solicit ethnic information. For example, there are applications on which you are
asked to indicate whether you are (or consider yourself to
be): American Indian, Black (Non-Hispanic), White (Non-
Hispanic), Hispanic, Puerto Rican, Alaskan Indian,
Asian, or Pacific Islander. If you are other than White
(Non-Hispanic), your application is likely to receive especially careful attention. The changes in social policy which
have given rise to this dramatic reversal of position on
identifying the ethnicity of applicants have been widely (if
rather uneasily) debated and need not be repeated here.

No single document is likely to reflect reality for long
but a report by the National Board on Graduate Education
(*Minority Group Participation in Graduate Education,*
1976) covers quite a bit of ground. It's available from the
National Academy of Sciences in Washington, D.C. or,
almost surely, from your reference librarian.

If you are a member of a minority group, this report is
worth examining but don't count on its being right up-to-
date. Ask your librarian if there are similar reports of more
recent date. Don't believe everything you read (what realist
would?) but some reading can help you adjust your campaign to the world that exists when you happen to be applying.

Other items of hard information such as honors, language facility, and the like I will treat as hard since I will
not advise you to lie outright. There is not much point in
outright lies about these matters since no one except a clerk
will even read what you've claimed. Certainly, it is ex-

tremely unlikely that those who actually make the decision about admitting you (i.e., faculty) will care in the slightest whether you've received the Aardvark Undergraduate Prize for Essays on the Fullness of Nothing—unless, perhaps, you're an English major.

There is, however, one item of hard information to which you should give the most careful attention. That item is the listing of your current telephone number. No matter how the request is phrased be certain that the number you enter is one at which you can be reached directly or by message during ordinary academic hours (i.e., 10:00 A.M. to 4:00 P.M.) in the period during which acceptance decisions will be made (roughly February 15 through May 15). If necessary, list two, three, or even four numbers to be certain that you'll be reachable during that period.

I'll explain the reasons for this compulsivity about telephone numbers when I discuss the real ins-and-outs of stipends. For now, make a note: don't take a chance with this item. It might prove to be costly if you list only the phone number for last semester's apartment.

The soft sections in this first part are those in which you are asked to (a) name your preferred academic advisor (PAA; see Glossary) at your target schools, and (b) write an autobiographical statement. All schools may not request both these items but that is irrelevant. You should provide them anyway since they constitute a major opportunity to shape the image you prefer.

Who is to say that this shaped image is false? Philosophers have been attempting for two thousand years to decide how one can know that something is true or false. You needn't worry about any breakthroughs occuring in your lifetime.

If you've appreciated my earlier descriptions of the

norms of academicians, you'll know that you'll depend on seeming to independently personify the values of your gatekeepers. Still, you're not dealing with the general case but, rather, with the case of specific individuals. How can you discover the values of some academician at a university 2,000 miles from your home, and years your senior in age?

Finding Names and Frogs of Various Sizes

Certainly the most revealing information is available on *big names* since these are individuals who have published page after page of papers and books. This is what has made them *big names* and the tips these writings will give you about the values of these movers and shakers in your target departments can't be overestimated. It is these *big names* who swing weight on departmental committees, in hiring decisions, and even—lest we forget—the type of graduate students in whom preferential interest is shown. Consequently, the sort of science, art, or scholarship in your target departments is powerfully shaped by the sort of scientist, artist, or scholar these *big names* believe themselves to be.

Even though these *big names* have spent all this time writing, you obviously do not want to spend a lot of time collecting and reading all of these pages. Still, you'll need to locate some of it and I'll tell you how to find *big name* publications in the process of identifying the *big names* in your home or target departments.

It is to be hoped that you are now able to work with the graduate school catalog received when you wrote for application materials and its list of faculty in the department of interest. If you received no such catalog, don't wait for a response to a letter asking for one. Check your own library since many have collections of these catalogs. Failing there, telephone the graduate school (not the target department) and ask for a catalog.

As a rule-of-thumb you will find no *big names* who are not listed as professors (as in *full professor*, although the adjective *full* is never used in printed formal material such as a catalog). The titles of professor, associate professor, assistant professor, instructor, and lecturer are merely labels of ranks (with professor being highest). That is, assistant professors do not assist professors nor, in cases where tenure comes before the promotion, do some associate professors any longer trouble to associate with professors. Nonetheless, it takes time in the harness to work up from assistant professor (the usual entry rank for a new Ph.D. at a university) to professor. So it is among those in this highest rank that you will find *big names*.

Of course, not all with the rank of professor are *big names*. It is a rare department with more than a few *big names* on its roster, and there probably will be more individuals than this holding the rank of professor in the department. However, eliminating some names by reason of rank immediately (associate professor and below) is advisable and you'll miss very few *big names*.

Your task is now to separate the *little names* from the *big names* on the list of professors in your home and target departments. It is very unlikely that there will be any *comer names* among the professors. Only those who have made it or settled into the genteel oblivion which marks the period between age forty and the retirement of the professorial *little name* are to be expected in this rank.

So, on the catalog list of full professors in your target department or on the *brag sheet* (see Glossary) many departments supply with application materials, look only at those identified with the sub-area in which you plan to study. This will still more sharply reduce the number of names of interest to you.

From this smaller list you might yourself recognize some names. Be very careful about using recognition to conclude the person is actually a *big name*. A familiar name might be that of a man who played second base for the Cubs when you were in grammar school. Moreover, even if the name is a scientist, artist, or scholar frequently mentioned by your undergraduate lecturers, the odds are better than even that such people are superannuated (a fancy word for "over the hill"). These *ex-big names* (see Glossary) are less useful for your purposes than *big names* who are currently active in the field. So, your own recognition of a name is an uncertain guide.

If you are applying for study in what are usually thought of as the sciences or social sciences, there are two different publications available at this writing that will let you assemble the journal publication lists of everyone in your target departments. (If you are applying in the humanities, a similar publication is in the works and may be out by the time you read this book. There are, however, alternative sources for publication information—listed in the back of this book in An Obscure Appendix—in the humanities, arts, and business categories that are almost as effortless to use as the two I'm about to describe.) The two now available are the *Science Citations Index* and the *Social Sciences Citation Index*. Both are published by the Institute for Science Information (ISI) of Philadelphia, Pennsylvania.

Both the ISI publications are issued periodically and cover all but the truly obscure journals in the science and social science fields. Both contain a section called a *corporate index*. This is an alphabetical listing *by the institution and department* with which cited authors are affiliated. Using the corporate index, all you need do is look up your home or target departments to find listed the names of every member who published anything in those hundreds of journals during the period covered.

To illustrate, suppose one of your target departments is the Martian Affairs Institute at Colombia University. Scanning the Cs in the corporate index of the SCI for 1978 you might find:

COLOMBIA UNIV, MART AFF INST, TUCSON, AR 16232, USA

SMYTH, D.	BONES AND BUGS	16 81 77
	RED PLANET	10 34 77
	MART CARTOG	18 23 77
WILSON, E. M.	HEAVENLY MARS	2 14 77
YOUNGER, T.	MART SCRIPT	6 19 77
	MART PRINT	8 23 77

Isn't that lovely? From this one entry you know that in the period covered, three people (Smyth, Wilson, and Younger) published articles in journals from *Bones and Bugs* to *Martian Printing*. You also have the exact citation (volume, page, and year) of each of those publications.

Go back, say, ten years while keeping score and you'll have compiled a list of who is and who is not publishing in the Martian Affairs Insititute. It's a piece of cake.

I hope you see the goal is to identify on your full professor lists those persons who practicing academicians in their sub-area *believe* to be big names. These beliefs are based on a number of things but all come down to two final factors: *Recognition status* and *in status* (see Glossary). These two factors themselves are based on some combination of number of publications through the years, presidencies of major professional associations, frequency of citation in papers written by others, and relative *hotness* (see Glossary) of the name's work at the moment or in the recent past. However, the single most important factor is number of publications.

The identification of *little names* is by a process of exclusion. They are the names remaining when *big names* have been identified. Generally speaking, the higher the academic rank of a *little name* the more appreciative he will be of signs that you recognize his existence. This may seem contrary to common sense but that is to ignore the conviction that grows steadily with the *little name's* age that his existence will have no lasting effect on anything once valued as a mark of achievement. There is a positive correlation between academic rank and age, so use rank if age information is not available. The rule here is: the higher the rank of a *little name,* the more battering his ego has taken and the more appreciative of any ego-oil you supply.

This method of identifying names of various sizes works exactly the same way for your home department. Just look up the faculty in the appropriate index and keep score. You'll need to know who's who when it comes to stalking those who will write letters of reference.

For those readers who will be aiming at a *lower* or *no class* department, very few *big names* and few *comer names* will be found to live there. They've already moved to fancier neighborhoods. In practice, this means that in such departments all faculty will be *little names* even though all will not have equal influence on matters affecting acceptance of students.

As always, you should fix your attention on those who identify themselves with your sub-area. If the faculty listing in the catalog does not help here, the *brag sheet* will usually be conclusive. Though all *little names*, there are nonetheless *big frogs* (all powerful) in *lower* or *no class* departments. You'll find it very useful to separate the *big frogs* from the others. Here are some things to consider as you examine the faculty names for this purpose in your target departments of these classes.

These departments tend to have a small number of faculty — in the neighborhood of twelve or less as a rule. These smaller departments are likely to operate as a single committee in deciding on admission of graduate students. The larger departments have long since been forced to create sub-area divisions or sections within the department to deal with regular administrative business. Still, as everywhere, the judgment of those faculty associated with the applicants' proposed study area will have a strong influence on the decision, particularly if those faculty are relatively senior (i.e., professors or associate professors).

I have only minor generalizations to offer about the importance of the chairman or head of these *lower* or *no class* departments. In some, this person wields almost dictatorial power and in others the department operates practically by referendum on every decision. I believe this variability is due indirectly to the smallness of the group and the absense of an internal bureaucratic structure. The result, then, reflects the style of the single individual who happens to be chairman or head.

Don't make the mistake of imagining that power automatically goes with the chairmanship or headship. That is, don't shape yourself for the departmental leader because of his title alone. At the same time, if the chairman or head is also identified with your sub-area, then he should definitely be treated as a *big frog* in your campaign.

Unlike *big names, big frogs* have not published sufficiently to help you get a fix on them. If they have published, they, like other *little names,* are more likely to have written reviews of books authored by others. Editors of periodicals that consist of (or, contain a few) book reviews in a given field are sometimes pressed to solicit these reviews from anyone since there's not much *career credit* (see Glossary) attached to writing reviews. The result is that this may be the main solution to the little name's problem of building up his publication list. Even though reviews don't count much, a list of them is better than an embarrassing blank space on the academician's curriculum vitae under the publications section.

Once again there is a simple way to discover if your names have written such book reviews. There are several alternatives listed in An Obscure Appendix but the one I believe most useful is titled *Current Book Review Citations* (New York: H. W. Wilson Co.). Issues are monthly. Each contains a cumulative record of citations in all *CBRC* volumes of reviews written by the alphabetically cited authors. More than 1,200 periodicals are examined by the Wilson search staff. Both fiction and non-fiction is covered, including science, law, children's, and young adult titles.

If you haven't time to actually look for these cited reviews in their published locations, you might instead examine the *Book Review Digest* (New York: H. W. Wilson Co.). This is also a monthly and lists authors alphabetically. It may be handy for someone pressed for time because it contains short excerpts from the actual reviews written by the listed authors.

While some will be *big frogs* in their own departments, they will usually be unknown to anyone in your home school. In that case, you may consult America's pale imitation of *Burke's Peers of the Realm*: the biographical directory in any one of its various forms. Again, your reference library is the place to find what you need.

The *Biographical Dictionaries Master Index* listed in An

Obscure Appendix will locate your names under any title. The sense of these titles comes down to "People in Science," or "American Artists Galore," or "Humanists in the USA." Each cover title tends to suggest that those listed are the VIPs of a given field of endeavor. Needless to say, you can't always tell a book by its cover.

Now that I've mentioned these *stud books* (see Glossary) you may wonder why I didn't recommend this source as a way of finding *big names* in all classes of departments. The explanation is simple even if somewhat damaging to certain illusions some people hold.

Specifically, such *stud books* do not necessarily contain the names and biographies of people that an independent group believes have accomplished something deserving of special notice. Rather, most of these directories contain information about people who have themselves been asked if they would care to be included! Some of them may be truly outstanding people but, on the other hand, a very large number are ego-trippers who rather fancy the idea that their names are to be found in a tome entitled "VIPs of Science." As a consequence, it is here you will surely find the *big frogs* in lesser class departments even if they are in the company of some truly accomplished people.

If it seems absurd to you that such directories are constructed from information in questionnaires that those listed take the time to complete, remember that these are merely directories. Those who consult them may have other illusions but the small print in the front matter of these commercial publications will contain a notice of the truth of the matter. Check it.

Still, you may be sure that no *big frog* breathes who does not complete each and every inquiring questionnaire for inclusion in these *stud books*.

All it ordinarily takes to receive such a questionnaire is to join a national professional association and these typically require only qualifications that are common among academicians in the field. It doesn't take long for the publishers who create these directories to acquire the names and addresses of new members of these associations.

Now, I'll summarize a bit and then press ahead. If you're aiming at *middle class* or *maximum class* departments, expect to find *big names* among the professors and *comer names* among the associate professors; expect also to find a number of *little names* intermixed with them in each rank.

If you're aiming at *lower* or *no class* departments, expect to find *big frogs* among the professors (or, if the department should have no full professors, among the associate professors). With rare exceptions all the names in these departments will be *little names* in their academic field however much weight they swing on their local turf.

You cannot spot *big frogs* by their publications (they are little names, remember, and haven't published much). Consultation of one or more biographical directory listing names of interest to you will identify them on a number of grounds. A *big frog* will have listed several officerships in state associations of professionals, a few articles in obscure journals, or have some sort of title in the department other than the title of academic rank. Titles are fascinating to *big frogs* and they seek them as predators their prey.

The dates of these officerships, obscure articles, and departmental titles are important to notice. *Big frogs* will have current departmental titles, a continuous history of various officerships in state associations, and a few outdated publications.

When you've found your *big frogs*, photocopy the biographical blurb in the stud book.

Your Tipster

At this point I must introduce you to your *tipster* (see Glossary). A *tipster* must be a faculty member in your home school in the sub-area to which you are applying for graduate study. He might be your academic advisor and, perhaps, you are best off if you happen to have an advisor who meets that qualification.

If your own advisor is not in your sub-area (it's not enough that he be a civil engineer if you're applying in fluid mechanics engineering), you should cultivate another person as your *tipster*. Obviously, you should in this case cultivate one as close to being in fluid mechanics as your home school provides. You decide who meets the qualifications and plan to tap what he knows about the reputations of your target school's *big names*.

Inducing your *tipster* to help you spot *big names* has been postponed to this point because it begins to merge into the topic of the next section on the pressure points of gatekeepers.

If you will consider the definition of a gatekeeper given in the Glossary, you'll see that his breed mainly includes those you want to write the sort of reference letters you prefer, those who have information you need to have, and those who will make decisions on your application. Since all of these individuals are academicians, they all will be moved by the same appeals. Whether tipster or advisor (and this might be the same person in your case) at your home school, or faculty member in the area in the target departments to which you apply, gatekeepers are all products of much the same academic rearing, the same occupational pressures, and of the same experiences with all those students who have come before you.

When you prepare to approach your *tipster* in your

home department, think of it as preparing for a trial run (but one with serious stakes, never forget) with the other gatekeepers you will later encounter. So, pay attention to your *tipster's* reactions as you seek to get him to share his beliefs about who's who.

You should first prepare a list of full professors associated with the sub-area in which you plan to study for your several target departments. You should now consult the index or abstract periodical in your field for the single most recent publication (paper, chapter, or book) authored by each of these people.

If the date of the most recent publication is more than five years in the past, the author is either a little name or an *ex-big name.* Five years may seem a short time but for the majority of academic journals there is at least a one-year publication lag. It would be a digression to explain the reasons for this delay between the date the editor first receives a manuscript and the date it appears in print but the lag is a fact of academic life. Therefore, the recommended five-year indicator of academic activity actually contains a hidden one-to-many year period on top of it.

If you are applying in a field in which the key activity is *making* or *doing* something (as opposed to publishing something), as in some of the fine arts, the five-year indicator is occasionally an uncertain guide to *little names* among full professors. Here, of course, the date of the last "single-artist exhibition" or recital tour should be noted, as should the regularity with which such activities have occurred over the years.

Those in the fine arts sometimes accord big name status to an artist who created or performed one particularly beautiful work or series of works in the distant past but has done little since then. Still, artists are academicians, too, and they are subject to the same "produce or perish" pressures that goad their colleagues in the sciences, humanities, business schools, engineering schools, medical schools, pharmacy schools, and agricultural schools. So, when in serious doubt, go with the five-year indicator in spotting *little name* full professors in the fine arts, too.

I'll avoid conjecturing on how much this vetting of your full-professor list will shrink the number of names that might remain. Actually, no one really knows how much dead wood there is here. The estimates vary according to whether the speaker is urging a reduction or increase in the budget of the university, school, department, or section in a given part of the education forest. There will be some shrinkage, though, and it will be the remaining names or *maybe big names* (see Glossary) that you will discuss with your *tipster*. These names will all be full professors in *middle class* or *maximum class* target departments who are associated with the sub-area in which you are applying for graduate study.

Those applying to lower-class departments in which only *big frogs* and other *little names* are to be found won't need to trouble with the following procedure. That may even be an advantage since it reduces the contacts with a tipster gatekeeper in which information is *solicited* (Principle 3).

Before approaching your tipster prepare a neatly typed listing of the maybe big names, grouping them under the heading of their respective universities (along with city and state of location except in cases of truly world-famous institutions). At minimum, double-space everything and, if necessary, cheat on the margins to keep it all on one page. You misspell a word or name on this list at your peril. Be sure to make a carbon copy for yourself. Do not attach an academic title (all professor anyway) or any other sort of title to any of these names. Do type your own name in a prominent location on the top of this page.

With list prepared, you'll make the first visit to your faculty *tipster's* office. Do try to visit during posted office hours since then your *tipster* has at least a minimum sense of obligation to pay attention to you. Some will even then seem inattentive but think how they'll act if you visit during a time not posted for student consultation.

The primary purposes of this visit are to inform your *tipster* that: (1) you're planning to apply to graduate school, (2) you've thought about particular schools, and (3) you've even troubled to find out something about them. This last may strike your *tipster* mute with astonishment; it will also sharply distinguish you from almost all of your compatriots-in-application.

Following civilities, remove your typed list from case or folder and hand it to your *tipster*. The note to strike here as you do so is that you are interested in these departments but need your *tipster's* guidance in judging their respective academic qualities. Be sure to suggest that you thought your *tipster's* evaluation of these faculty members would be one way to do that.

Note my stress on "guidance" and "evaluation" here. These are two invaluable words for use by students in *tipster* contacts. The former is used whenever the student wishes to induce an especially superior attitude in a *tipster*. This attitude always makes *tipsters* feel good, so induce it as often as possible without appearing obsequious. The other word, "evaluation," is used whenever the student wishes to encourage a *tipster* to gossip about anything. Academicians love to gossip so cue them regularly with "evaluation" requests.

Your *tipster* — as an individual whom you will ultimately (but not on this first contact) ask to write a letter of recommendation for you — is a gatekeeper. The gate is opened by creation of a sense of personal relationship with you. This first contact with your *tipster* (advisor or not) in context of application to graduate school should be fairly brief, well-organized by your preparation, and respectful of the status your *tipster* surely imagines due him.

Some things to remember are these. Always address your *tipster* as Doctor, or (more safely) as Professor—whether or not this is actually the tipster's title. Even if, in a burst of democratic generosity, your *tipster* should ask you to use a "first name" be sure to slip back often to the Doctor or Professor title. Avoid "Sir" or, at all costs, "Madam," or any variant of it. The former is rather old-fashioned and the latter is loaded with social dynamite.

You are not trying to become your *tipster's* buddy; you are trying to stand out from the mass of your compatriots and create the feeling that you recognize your *tipster's* status. If you should study social psychology you would learn that this is attempting to trade on the "norm of distributive justice" but that's just *clubspeak* for giving your *tipster* his due in the expectation of receiving your due (e.g., a friendly attitude) in return.

Ask your *tipster* if he would care to keep your list in order to think it over, saying that you could return another time. This will trigger him to get down to business and give you the "evaluations" you seek. Take notes! In your own notebook!

One might think that having someone take notes of an academician's remarks would be so common an experience (all those endless lectures, and such) as to have no effect on these worthies. Nothing could be further from the truth concerning notes taken outside the lecture room.

I have seen the most indifferent of lecturers (inside the lecture room) display eager—almost maternal—concern that each thought be captured completely when notes are made of their remarks outside the lecture room. I was present when one colleague even offered to read over the notes the student visitor to his office had made to be sure that nothing had been missed. He really wanted to be helpful!

You are there to listen — not to talk. Answer direct questions, of course, and be ready to supply your neatly typed curriculum vitae (described in chapter four, Taming the Wild Reference) if your *tipster* begins to ask questions about your past academic work, but otherwise, listen.

Think of it this way. All academicians love to talk. Your *tipster* is an academician. Therefore, your *tipster* loves to talk. Don't interfere.

In the course of commenting on the *maybe big names* and their respective departments, your *tipster* will naturally spend most of the time talking about (a) the higher class departments, (b) the true *big names* on the list, and (c) trivia of an unbelievable variety.

Don't force attention to each name. If your *tipster* doesn't mention one or more of the *maybe big names,* they are probably little names. On rare occasions, a *tipster* may say quite honestly that a name is unknown to him. Needless to say, this is probably a little name. Keep score in your notes.

You, of course, should express no opinion whatsoever except understanding and appreciation. If it fits your style, the phrase "I see" is absolutely marvelous for accomplishing this.

When you think you have what your *tipster* has to give, do not linger unless it is utterly clear that your *tipster* wants you to stay. With thanks and some piety to the effect that you appreciate your *tipster's* guidance — get the hell out!

You may be tempted to impress your *tipster* with words suggesting your devotion to studies, your lifelong ambition to be a researcher, or your general sophistication. If so, don't give in to temptation. Your *tipster* has heard it all before (many times). It will be your actions that are impressive in the beginning since they will distinguish you from other students your *tipster* has known. Words are, indeed, of lesser value since they might suggest that you're working at impression management (Principle 4).

The Pressure Points of Gatekeepers

A pressure point here (by analogy with the same term used in Red Cross First Aid courses) refers to a contact point that, if pressed, interferes with the flow of something (not blood, in this case). That "something" is a grooved (or stereotyped) impression of you, your abilities, and your potential.

Whether in connection with *tipsters*, academic advisors, reference letter writers, or target department gatekeepers, you must interfere with the stereotyped impression they will have of you based on your similarities with the long line of undergraduates whom they've previously encountered. You must strive to appear dissimilar from your compatriots—but only along approved dimensions. That is, strive to be *OK-different* (see Glossary). As you press on these (approved) dissimilarities, you will interrupt the stereotyped reaction to you. Once you've done that, you'll have taken the first step toward becoming an identifiable person who will receive treatment as an individual.

From first to last the most important image to reinforce in the minds of all of your gatekeepers is that of a person who is always prepared and organized. So few undergraduates whom academicians encounter are prepared and organized that this impression alone will carry you far in generating your unique identity. You will thereby benefit from what social psychologists call a *contrast* effect. That is, anything which is even moderately better than what your gatekeepers firmly expect will be thought to be exceptionally superior.

Part of the preparation and organization you will display will be unavoidably apparent to your home school gatekeepers when you reach the stage of seeking letters of reference from them. Part of it will be displayed to your target schools in the autobiographical statement you'll construct for each. However, in both cases, this should be a display in passing—a display that is apparent but only so because the questions you ask, the lists you present, your letters, and the like will be such that they could only have originated from an individual who is prepared and organized.

Recall Principle 4—*effortful* impression management is bad impression management. He manages best who seems not to be working at it.

In your campaign, you will seem to be working at something else in what is no more than an efficient manner. However, because this itself is such an unusual manner, your image as an identifiable individual who is *OK-different* will come into existence.

Another pressure point that will interrupt the assignment of you to that vague category of "a letter I have to write" or "an application I have to read" is reached by some sort of out-of-channels contact with the gatekeeper. There are limits here, of course, and I strongly advise against dropping in at your gatekeeper's home Sunday afternoon when he is burning hamburgers for his family.

There is one exception to this general rule of avoiding gatekeeper contacts outside of campus settings. There do exist faculty members who encourage all sorts of informal out-of-channels contact with graduate students and, for that matter, with undergraduate students as well.

These faculty are generally young, were degreed in the informal sixties, and tend to be more heavily concentrated in the social sciences and the humanities. They want to be viewed as gurus who are in touch with their students. If you see signs that some gatekeeper wants that sort of relation with students, cooperate by all means.

Some signs of this sort of desire are:

— the faculty member chooses to eat lunch in the dining hall or campus restaurant where more students than other faculty usually are to be found. If there is only one lunch place on your campus, a potential gatekeeper who sits with students rather than with other faculty can be cultivated if you simply begin to have your lunch in the vicinity and gradually work your way into his varied collection of student followers.

— the faculty member chooses to wear informal clothing when most faculty wear neckties, cultured pearls, or other items of more formal clothing. Ragged "tennies" or running shoes are a dead giveaway.

— the faculty member chooses to use campus slang in conversations with students. Such usage must be more than a few words since some of the stuffiest faculty will occasionally use a slang word or two that they fancy will establish their awareness of contemporary student affairs. In such cases, you can practically hear the quotation marks drop into place around the slang words, so it's easy to steer clear of these people.

The varieties of out-of-channels contacts that are possible with faculty who want to be people of the people include Friday afternoon beer sessions, noon-hour sports, and weekend gatherings. You, as an undergraduate, will undoubtedly underestimate the readiness of such faculty to allow you to insert yourself into such activities. All I can tell you is that you cannot overestimate the importance of having followers to such faculty members, and if you're willing to be a good follower (i.e., one who visibly appreciates the brilliance of the leader), you'll be very welcome.

Even if you're restricted to on-campus contacts with your gatekeepers, you are not limited to their offices, classrooms, or notes in their mailboxes.

There are three types of settings other than these that are all the more effective for an identity builder's purposes because they are not exploited by others. There is nothing intrusive about carefully prearranged (however seemingly accidental) encounters. How much trouble you may care to take in exploiting them, I cannot say. Each has been tested in my own or others' experience, however, so I can recommend them to that extent. Each setting lends itself more naturally to different purposes in identity building, though, so exploitation of each should be adjusted to fit the need.

Campus Environment Contacts

Since most academicians give very little attention to the identity (i.e., name, face, circumstances) of a student who is not involved in something of interest to the academician, they must be given practice to fix the necessary facts in mind.

It is not true that simply attending a class for a semester will serve to even associate your face with the correct name in the memory of your instructor. Even if you manage to pose some incisive question to him at regular intervals during the semester, the best you can probably hope is that you will become a familiar stranger.

In class, he will recognize you (sans name, in most cases). On campus he might recognize you as a present or past student (or, perhaps, an advisee). If he sees you off campus he will perhaps wonder for a few seconds where he's seen you before. Since you'll profit from a more specific identity than this, here are some ideas about ways to become real to him through on campus contacts.

Academicians are creatures of habit; some routines are imposed on them by class schedules, some by lunch hours, and some by personal devotions such as jogging, tennis, or other currently faddish exercise activities. The point is that the most cursory observations will reveal times of day when you can be virtually certain of meeting any given home-school gatekeeper on the way to or from one of these various activities. Given this, it is a trivial problem for you to arrange to encounter a gatekeeper a few times (with a simple, "Hello, Professor Jones," in passing) in days *before* and *after* a first meeting in Professor Jones's office where your actual identity can be made known. That's part of what I meant about giving a gatekeeper practice in identifying you.

I cannot even estimate the number of times I (or colleagues) have been greeted by a student while crossing the campus with the almost invariable effect that (when the student is out of earshot) the one greeted says something such as "That's a student in my introductory course," or 'He's my undergrad advisee," or, even, "That's a good student — always asks the right questions in my class." These remarks help to fix your identity in the speaker's mind.

A student's act of greeting in an out-of-channels setting has the most amazing effect of enhancing his recognizability. Indeed, there have been times when I have — following such a greeting — suddenly (it seemed) become aware of seeing a particular student everywhere I happened to go. Now, perhaps those students had anticipated my advice here and had actually arranged all those far-flung encounters with me. Whether they did or not, those greetings did draw my attention to them sufficiently to markedly increase my sense of knowing them.

The beneficial effects on a student's image following judicious encounters with some gatekeeper in places such as the library, the computer center, or the halls of research areas (it is irrelevant that the student is *not* involved in any research; the gatekeeper won't know the difference) cannot be overestimated. These are out-of-channels contacts exactly because most faculty gatekeepers truly do not expect to see the typical undergraduate in them. Hence, such encounters will help to set you apart as an *OK-different* individual.

You can even use a seemingly accidental campus encounter to begin to associate your name with your face. It's not useable more than once but it can be followed by other campus and office contacts to assist a gatekeeper's generally inadequate memory for such details.

The approach here may seem bold but it is quite safe. Suppose, for example, that an important gatekeeper is a computer-user. Knowing this, you might stop him (never when he has company) in the corridor near his office with words to the following effect.

"Hello, Professor Zahler. I've seen you in the computer center and I was wondering whether you cover computer applications in [the gatekeeper's field] in any of your advanced undergraduate courses? My name's Sam Student."

There are several things to note about this greeting. First, it incorporates the gatekeeper's name (and title, whether or not he actually is a full professor). It also suggests that Sam Student himself is a habitué of the computer center but doesn't make any specifically time-bound claims. It emphasizes that Sam is a serious student interested in Zahler's *advanced* courses. Lastly, Sam's self-introduction comes at the end — after the gatekeeper's attention has been caught.

All in all, it's an efficient package and the gatekeeper can fabricate all sorts of answers that sound rational so there is no possibility of embarassing him. Morevoer, the gatekeeper's answer can be brief or detailed, depending on his preferences or schedule. He may even invite Sam to visit his office to discuss the matter further. Whatever happens, Sam Student will begin to become a real person with a name.

Other contacts in other settings will be necessary but this can be an effective inital opening. This, of course, follows from the fact that Sam approaches as a supplicant (*never* as a peer) and gives the gatekeepr an opportunity to say almost anything that enters his head. Academicians thrive on such things. The only mistake Sam can make is to take more of the gatekeeper's time than he wants to give at that moment.

Some useful variants of this ploy, depending on circumstances, would be as follows.

"Hello, Professor Hummer. I've taken your introductory course and I wanted to ask for your advice on which *advanced* course in [the gatekeeper's field] you think I should take next. My name is Sam Student." If the class is large it doesn't matter whether Sam has actually taken this course.

"Hello, Professor Maven. I've been doing some extra reading in [the gatekeeper's field] and I wanted your advice on which advanced course I should take first. My name is Sam Student." Again it doesn't matter whether Sam has done this reading as long as he's memorized the author and title of one book in the field in case he's asked.

"Hello, Professor Macher. My advisor suggested I ask your advice about some areas for extra reading in [gatekeeper's field]. My name is Sam Student." Here, too, it

matters not whether Sam's advisor has ever mentioned the
subject; he wouldn't remember anyway.

Notice that all of these variants reflect Sam's supposed
interest in the gatekeeper's field and all are phrased so they
neither commit Sam to doing something definite nor require the gatekeeper to make any commitment to do anything. The purpose is to begin to associate Sam's name and
desired image with his face—not to involve Sam or the
gatekeeper in doing something that neither of them wants
(or has the time) to do.

It's understandable for several reasons that even those
who appreciate the importance of achieving some identity
in their gatekeepers' minds do not often make such contacts as these. Most prominent among these reasons is that
students often think of faculty gatekeepers as alien beings
who might react in some unpredictable and undesirable
way to such approaches. We are generally more comforta-
ble with people who are similar to ourselves in part because
we think we know how they'll react when we deal with
them. Faculty gatekeepers are—it is thought by students—so different than they that there is no telling what
will happen if a student does or asks anything out of the
ordinary. The result is that even with some choice in the
matter students minimize almost all out-of-channels contact with faculty gatekeepers.

There are, of course, many ways in which faculty gatekeepers do differ from students. However, they are merely
different, not alien. Their pressure points are those of a
group of people who are the end result of a process of self-
selection as well as environmental selection that began
anywhere from four to forty years in the past; as individuals they are still human for all that.

In this connection you should expect to find that if you

have never done any of the following you are probably indistinguishable from all of your undergraduate classmates:

— asked carefully respectful questions of an instructor following his lectures.

— greeted an instructor by name in some setting other than a classroom or the instructor's office.

— visited an instructor's office in the semester *following* the one in which you took his course to tell him how much you enjoyed his course.

— asked for an instructor's advice about readings in his field that are not otherwise required in his own or some other course.

— asked an instructor about the nature of his research or writing or thinking in his own sub-area.

— asked for an instructor's advice about what courses to take in his field.

The list could be extended but I think the point is clear. Each of these actions works to separate you from the crowd and none require that you actually commit yourself to doing anything. Think of it as investing in an odd sort of savings account. The principal is useless to you but the interest will be there for withdrawal when you need it.

Independent Readings and Research

There is no more powerful means open to an undergraduate for transforming himself into an indentifiable individual in the minds of gatekeepers at his home school than these tutorial courses. Such a course is customarily arranged with an individual faculty member according to his willingness to accept a particular student in any given semester.

At many private colleges and universities, there is greater emphasis on such courses than at most public institutions.

Still, even at publilc institutions such course opportunities are nearly universal in the catalogs. It's up to the individual student to capitalize on those opportunities.

Unlike the identity-enhancing contacts discussed under Campus Environment Contacts, exploiting these tutorial courses will require some commitment by you to actually do something. What's more, once committed, you *must* do it or you'll have done far more harm than good. It will also be necessary (usually) to arrange with an individual faculty member in the preceding semester to take such a course with him and that means some planning. Nonetheless, there are still options that you can select to control how much (and what kind of) doing will probably be involved.

The Coolie Option

This refers to any arrangement in which you assist your potential gatekeeper in some aspect of his own or his graduate students' research. I've called this the "Coolie Option" since such an undergraduate assistant will be asked to do any work that neither the faculty member nor any graduate students working with him wants to do. If you choose the Coolie Option you will not be required to do any thinking (or much writing) even though your transcript will probably note that you received credit for independent research. You will also probably get an A grade in this course providing only that you've been diligent in doing what someone has told you to do.

Anything-You-Say Option

You might choose this more adventuresome option. Unlike the Coolie Option, this may be open to you under either an independent readings or independent research course title. The "You" in "Anything You Say" is the faculty member whom you are cultivating, say, as a potential source of a reference letter—not you, the person who should eagerly follow whatever lead he gives.

All you must do here is start the ball rolling by approaching him to ask if he would be willing to take you in an independent course so that you can (do) (read about) some research in his field. You need not have any sort of original question or idea about what you want to do but that's not important. For example, I've had students say they wanted to study something with me that I am almost positive was a rephrasing of some end-of-chapter discussion question in the textbook I use in my own introductory course in social psychology.

The important thing is that you should begin by saying "I want to study or read more about X" where X is somewhere in the faculty member's general area of interest. That way, no matter how he modifies your project—as he almost certainly will—it will be partly your idea.

From there you need only follow his lead, take careful notes of what he says, and he will wind up doing all the planning while imagining himself to be assisting you to focus your thinking. Of course, you should then simply do anything he suggests you do. If he gives you choices, wait one day, ask for his advice on the choice, and he'll make the choices for you. It happens all the time.

I'd Rather Do It Myself

This can be a very time-consuming option. I do not advise choosing this option. To be sure, there will be the most powerfully positive effects on your image and identity if you manage to bring it off but the cards are stacked against you. It will take a great deal of work, and, perhaps most important, you will be faced with the recurrent problem of tactfully doing something other than what your supervising gatekeeper suggests.

Suppose, for example, you've arranged to do some sort of empirical investigation on a topic of interest to you in your instructor's field. Without even specifying that field, I know your instructor will believe you have already made the following "mistakes":

— the question you are addressing is too broad.

— you have not conceptualized the question in terms of any of several relevant theories.

— your knowledge of the relevant literature is inadequate.

— you have no good idea of how to study your question.

— the required support apparatus or assistance is not available to you.

— you do not have the skills to analyze the results of your investigation.

What's more, your instructor will in almost all cases be correct in these beliefs. However, even if he is not correct, he will believe that he is and, having chosen this option, you must then deal with resisting his advice to modify your plans without offending him. I have known students to be successful but I would remind you that one reason you've taken on this project is to cultivate — not alienate — your gatekeeper. It's not a good bet, typically, that you'll be able to walk this line successfully.

Phone Calls and Personal Interviews

These are out-of-channels contacts that are equally useful with your home school and your target school gatekeepers. However, since these contact are often all that can be practically exploited with target school gatekeepers, I'll describe them in that context. The purpose is the same in either context, though — to become a real individual who is *OK-different* in the minds of your gatekeepers.

It's understandable that if you're reluctant to intrude on your home school gatekeepers, you'll feel even more uneasiness about making an out-of-channels contact with faculty members at your target schools. Again, it's that old devil uncertainty: how will this total stranger react? Isn't it better to keep a low profile? What good will it do anyway?

Of course you'll ask yourself these questions; it is human to do so. It's the answers that you give yourself that can lead you to separate yourself from the mob and acquire an identity of your very own.

The very first truth to accept, though, is that the individual faculty members serving in whatever sort of admissions group exists in your target department will not be mortally offended if you telephone to ask the sorts of questions I'll describe for you. They have received such calls before (although not in large numbers, to your good fortune) and most of them will believe that there are good reasons for your contacts. I hope you noticed that I referred to individual faculty members here because another thing you should realize is that these are the people who actually make the decision about accepting you.

It is not the graduate school (or any dean or director in it), nor is it a department head (in almost all cases), nor is it anyone in the central administration of the target university (such as a provost, or chancellor, or a vice-president for academic affairs or anyone in their offices). These various offices and officers may rubber-stamp acceptances that are made by various admissions committees but the decisions that count have already been made. Of course, some of the official correspondence you'll receive will bear the names of administrative officers but the decision about an individual graduate-school applicant is almost certainly a faculty decision. Graduate school is completely different from undergraduate school in this matter. In graduate school, an admissions officer signs papers but does not make decisions about whom to admit.

Obviously, then, your telephone or interview contacts should be with faculty members. Having an indentity with them will make a difference that matters. Even if you have quite ordinary credentials, you'll receive more consideration if you have become a real person to one or more faculty decision-makers. Most academicians privately believe that they themselves are better judges of a student's potential than any collection of transcripts and multiple-choice test scores.

When a first telephone contact should be made can be determined from your target school's published dates for final submission of an application. A general estimate is to take that date and subtract three-and-a-half months. If the final date is June 1, a first call could be made on February 15. I'll explain some of the reasons for this estimate when I describe the real ins-and-outs of stipends in the last chapter.

Some of your target schools may have instructed you to send all parts of your application package to a specified office in the graduate school. Others may have directed you to send parts (such as reference letters) to the department to which you're applying and the rest (application form, transcripts, GRE scores) straight to the graduate school. Either way, you should feel no concern about contacting an individual faculty member for fear that he won't know anything about your application. You don't care if he knows anything about the papers you've submitted! You can tell him everything necessary (i.e., that you are applying and your name).

Obviously, you should not be so crude as to come right out and say that you're calling in order to become an identifiable person. Rather, you might adopt one of the following lines of rationalization for your first telephone contact. Incidentally, here's where you can make use of the inside information that you have collected on your target school gatekeepers.

Your Name Is a Legend

"I'm working on a [senior thesis; literature review; paper] having to do with your research area, and I called to ask if there were papers you've written beyond those I've located on [whatever it is]. My advisor suggested that I call to ask you whether there are. My name is Sam Student."

This is a ploy that may test your skills to a greater extent than others but if you can bring it off it will have a dynamite impact on the target school gatekeeper. He'll probably even find some way to brag to his colleagues about your request — to your benefit, needless to say. After all when undergraduates are directed to one's work, can legendary fame be far behind?

Your opening request did not, please note, include the information that you are an applicant. Wait until your telephonic target responds and then work that into your conversation with him. The opening you've given him will elicit some kind of response. You want to be sure he's finished thinking about what he's going to say before you give him the key identity information. Otherwise he might not get it into his ears, to say nothing of his memory.

Contrary to what you might imagine, this approach can be used with any potential gatekeeper who has published anything, anywhere, and at any time (providing only that you have located at least one of those published articles).

If your target is an individual who hasn't published for years, he will be gratified that someone — even an undergraduate — still knows about him. If your target has had only scattered publications in obscure journals over the years, you can be virtually certain that he has a number of papers that he thinks should have been published by the major journals in his field but were not because of editorial stupidity alone. If your target has a very recent publication, he'll be able to rummage through his memory for earlier papers that he fancies to be related somehow or, perhaps, tell you about a paper presently being prepared for publication. If your target has a zillion publications, he's a *big name* who might not remember you no matter what you do. Still, he might keep you in mind long enough to speak your name to his secretary as he gives directions to send you a few reprints of his papers.

That brings me to a point that is relevant here though I'll discuss it in more detail in the next section. You might have already learned that some number of reprints of an article are supplied the author of an academic paper by the journal or periodical that publishes it. If not, then know now that some number between fifty and one hundred reprints are supplied to the author. The purpose of creating these reprints is that they may be sent to those who ask for them.

While you might (as I've said) know this, you almost surely do not know that even articles that do *not* make it into print probably exist in some smaller number in what is called *pre-print* form. A pre-print is simply a mimeo, ditto, or, perhaps even, photocopy version of the article that was (or, is to be) submitted for possible publication by some journal. These pre-prints were created by the author to distribute among his friends for critical comment before submitting the paper to a journal, and in the anticipation of a flood of requests from the famous specialists in his field who might learn of his work through the professional gossip network.

Since every author will almost certainly overestimate the number of copies of such pre-prints that will be needed for these purposes, you will be sent pre-prints, if you express interest. It's not even a big deal; just go ahead and ask about pre-prints when you make your first telephone contact with a target school gatekeeper. You'll not only get them if he has them, it'll give you a chance to tell him the name of your home university or college when you give your campus address.

Every bit of identifying information you work in will help you. Your undergraduate school's name may help to distinguish you among the other applicants when this gatekeeper eventually gets down to making his share of the acceptance decision with his faculty colleagues.

After your target has finished what he has to say about his past, present, and future publications, you should thank him for the information, mentioning that you've applied for graduate study in his department although you know of course that final decisions haven't been made.

Don't push or even hint at pushing on where you stand at this point. Just conclude the conversation politely with the private hope that you've left some part of your identity in his mind as an applicant who is *OK-different*. You don't have a face yet but you are beginning to be more than a set of papers.

If he does send you anything, fire back an immediate letter in which you thank him briefly for taking interest in your project. He probably hasn't but your letter is one more bit of identifying contact with an individual who will soon be deciding the fate of your application. Type neatly and, for your own sake, spell all the words correctly; it could be death if you don't since on such tiny bases, lasting first impressions are formed.

If you have already written (or can modify) a paper that refers to your target school gatekeeper's work in some ap-

propriately adulatory way, wait one week and send him a
copy with a brief covering letter thanking him for his interest in your project.

Be careful here, though. While chances are that he will
do no more than skim it (looking for his own name, probably), he might actually read it. Just on the off-chance that
he does read it, you'll want to be very sure that it's typed
neatly, and that the words are both used and spelled correctly. The content is much less important providing you
haven't said anything that is incorrect about the
gatekeeper's views. Long quotations from his published
papers are the best defense against this fatal error.

Short of sending a paper, send him a short letter in
which you thank him for taking an interest in your project.
Since you should have actually read one or more of his
publications, try to mention some tidbit from his articles
that led to your interest in further study of the question or
problem if you send only a letter. For example, look in the
conclusion or summary sections for questions he raised,
or — to be really fancy — compare several of his other
papers of about the same date to find some common
theme. An army may, as Napoleon supposedly said, travel
on its stomach but an academician travels on his intellectual ego. You should be trying to encourage him to invite
you along on his trip. You may be sure that he loves admir-
ing company.

Satan Is Tempting Me

This telephonic contact will be useful for establishing
your identity as well as for finding out where your application stands or discovering what stage deliberations have
reached on applications. It is less time-consuming than the
"Your Name Is a Legend" approach and might even sug-

gest the counterproductive idea that you do not fully appreciate your role as a supplicant. So, handle it with care.

The idea here is to strongly imply that some other graduate program has already accepted you at the time of your phone call. You are, then, trying to find out about how long it will be until your gatekeeper's department will make a tentative decision about your application.

You should never volunteer the name of the other school; that is very bad form, even if another school has actually acccepted you for graduate study. You will probably not be asked directly to name this other school since that, too, is bad form.

If you should be asked merely say "Oh, it's another good school across the country," and only the most crude of academicians will pursue the question (even though those who don't pursue it will be dying to know). In any event, whatever you say will never be checked for accuracy.

The timing of this contact is important if it is to yield you maximum benefits and information. To estimate the best timing requires that you know some facts about the typical process of dealing with graduate applications in schools granting academic degrees (*not* professional degrees such as in medicine or law).

There are, of course, some few departments that are as systematic about making this decision as they all pretend to be. Such exceptional departments will present you fewer problems in finding out when decisions happen because (1) a planned system exists, and (2) that system is followed by the committees of faculty members who make decisions on admissions. These departments are perhaps also less influencible by impression management on your part but there are certainly no data on this score. Anyway, such departments are surely relatively few in number so, since it won't hurt anything, you can proceed as if they do not even exist.

The key assumptions you should take as generally true are these:

—application materials that you send to the graduate school receive only minimal processing there. Little more than notation of receipt of the required parts and comparison with the published minimum grade averages or scores for eligibility will be made by a clerk in the graduate school.

—materials received by the graduate school are then shipped to the department to which you have applied for acceptance. A secretary will accumulate these materials in your file until all required have been received.

—the many applications to that department will slowly grow complete. Depending on the size (i.e., number of faculty) of the department one of three sorts of things will happen next.

—if the department is very small (fewer than ten faculty members), the department chairman or head will begin prodding his colleagues to read all these applications in preparation for a meeting to discuss admissions. Even in such small departments, the faculty who specialize in the sub-area of interest to given applicants will accord those applications their primary attention and other faculty will generally defer to their opinions.

—if the department is middle-sized (between about ten and thirty faculty members), there will probably be some sort of internal administrative structure such that groups of faculty in different broadly designated speciality areas will be responsible for applications to each area. As applications begin to accumulate, the individuals who have been roped into looking after admissions in each area will begin to prod their colleagues to read their "own" applications in preparation for a meeting to discuss admissions.

—if the department is large (thirty faculty members on up to the giants of one hundred that do, in fact, exist), there may be some sort of sub-sub-area organization (often called "programs" and responsible for their very own applicants) *within* the different broadly-designated speciality areas that will certainly exist as administrative units. These broader areas will surely have designated heads and, as the number of faculty in them increases, regularly take on many of the features of a department within a department (many large biology departments, for example, are composed of sections, each with heads, executive officers, and all the outward signs of separate departments).

—whatever the case, the *total number in the group of faculty members who will actually decide on your application will be small.* If you can become a promising real person to only one or two of this group your leverage will be enormous no matter what the overall size of the department.

—the schedule followed by these decision-making groups in acting on applications will vary by two weeks to two months between departments in the same as well as different schools but there are some constraints that control all departments. These constraints are imposed by the desire in all departments to get the good students among their applicants.

The purpose of the "Satan Is Tempting Me" approach is to appear to be seeking some understandable clarification about the decision-making schedule of your target department while, in fact, establishing your identity in the mind of a gatekeeper in those departments. This approach can be used with one member of a given target department while the "Your Name Is a Legend" approach is being used with another gatekeeper in that same department.

One variation involves calling the chosen gatekeeper,

and saying simply that you have applied to the department, are still interested in studying there but wonder if you can get an estimate of a decision period since you've "had a response from another school."

Needless to say, this will be the literal truth since you will have had at least two "responses" from every school to which you have applied. One of those responses was made when each sent you the application forms you requested and one was a routine acknowledgement that all of your application materials had been received. Admittedly, in the context of this conversation with a gatekeeper, he will undoubtedly presume that this "response" was an acceptance to graduate study but it's not your problem if he jumps to this incorrect conclusion.

If you prefer a different form of the "Satan Is Tempting Me" approach of establishing an identity, you might trouble to apply to some department that is so certain to admit you that your use of the past tense (i.e., "*had* a response") is an unimportant detail arising from the fact that you are calling in late February rather than in late May (by which time you will certainly have *had* an acceptance from this dead cinch *insurance school).*

In these, as in other versions of the "Satan Is Tempting Me" contact, the opening of the conversation is to (1) establish your identity in an understandable context and (2) establish the idea that your body has value elsewhere. That other department which values you is Satan.

This is not — and cannot be — an image-building contact to be pressed beyond the mildly suggestive. Although you do hope to get information of use in controlling your own jitters over when you can expect to hear something about your application, don't lose sight of the importance of working your name and home school into the conversation. You'll have wasted your time if the gatekeeper to whom you talk doesn't retain some association between your call and your application when he eventually reads it or, even, reconsiders it.

Here are two ways of getting your name across without being too obvious about being more interested in that than anything else:

—ask to leave your name and an additional telephone number (not included on your application form) where you can sometimes be reached during the next few weeks. Be certain you emphasize that this is an *additional* number and that those on the application are the main numbers. Enlist a good friend to volunteer his number but don't expect any messages there because the gatekeeper will misplace the note he makes of the additional number. Your only concern anyway is with a plausible justification for saying—and spelling—your name.

—ask if he has received a paper you've written and sent him "last week" as an addition to your application credentials. A minor paper you wrote for an undergraduate course and refurbished for this use in building your identity will be sufficient. When he says he hasn't received it you will surely have a chance to supply your name and the title of the paper.

The "Satan Is Tempting Me" ploy should not be used so early in the season during which applications are being considered that it is implausible for another school to have accepted you. However, there is sufficient variability between departments in any field in acting on applications that none of your gatekeepers is likely to know for sure when other departments are making decisions. So, you'll be safe using this ploy during the month of February onward. Obviously, the closer in time you use it to the decision-making period, the more likely a gatekeeper will remember you when it counts. I would advise you to fix on

the last week in February as a good time to make this sort
of call.

In addition, if you wish you can adapt this ploy to
your use in the middle of March if you still haven't heard
from some department in which you are especially interested.

By that time, you are probably (but not certainly, by any
means) too late to benefit from the identity-building effects of the ploy. However, you might move your target
department gatekeeper to tell you that:

—all "first round" acceptances have been issued but
those invited have not all decided whether they are coming.

—you are in a "second round" category of applicants
and might be accepted if some other student declines to
come. If so, you're still in the game.

—there is no hope for your application but you'll probably not be notified until "the secretaries catch up with
their work." Curiously, it is always the fault of secretaries
that such no-thank-you notes haven't been sent.

Actually, no matter what your gatekeeper may say here,
there is still some possibility that you might eventually
receive an acceptance of your application. There are
several reasons for this:

—all departments will accept all the *superpersons* and
many of the *solidpersons* who have applied. There are only
so many such people to go around in many fields so, until
cloning techniques are more advanced, many departments
will be turned down by applicants who are going elsewhere.

—since "first round" applicants may take weeks to
notify the various departments that they are not coming
(and some applicants never do so), many of a given department's "second round" applicants will have accepted offers

from other schools where they were "first round" choices.

— more than a little panic can result when a department begins to learn that some of its own "second round" applicants have already decided to go elsewhere by the time the department gets around to trying to replace its first round choices who have declined.

— this panic at the prospect of having too few incoming graduate students may stimulate a department to reassess the applications of those who were previously not even second-round choices.

If your application happens to be one of those that were previously unappreciated, any last minute attention you've given to identity-building will assist you in rising to a more appreciated status when and if such panic strikes your target departments.

I'm Coming

205263

The personal interview is the very best means open to you for establishing your identity with target department gatekeepers. It is also a superb means of cultivating home school gatekeepers but I'll return to that in the chapter on stalking references.

Obviously, unless you happen to be ridiculously wealthy you will not be able to afford the expense of traveling to schools far from your home grounds. Still, if there is any way that you can arrange to get to a school where you plan to (or have) applied, you should do it. If you can't reach all your target departments, reach the ones you can. It's the best way of putting a face on your name, and gatekeepers are definitely affected by names with faces more than they are by papers with names.

Having identified your gatekeeper you should call him at least ten days before you hope to visit and ask if it would be possible for you to come talk to him about "the graduate program" in his department. Follow his lead and his convenience but if you put it to him that you are planning to visit his campus on a certain day, he is very likely to succumb to your request to talk to him. If he says he's going to be out of town that day, ask if there is another day you might see him since you "think it would be possible to change your schedule" for visiting his campus. If he waffles still, forget him because he really doesn't want to see you and you'll make matters worse by pressing. Just pick another gatekeeper in that department and call him with the same pitch.

Assuming you get someone to agree to see you, follow up immediately with a letter in which you thank him for agreeing to see you on a certain date. If you can manage to get letterhead paper of your school from a friendly source (ask a graduate teaching assistant or a sympathetic young instructor), use it for this or any other letters to individual gatekeepers. There is no impropriety here. You've certainly paid enough in tuition and fees to your home school in four years to justify a few sheets of letterhead typing paper for this clearly educational purpose. The idea is that such paper may subtly imply to the recipient that you are on the "inside" at your home school.

In fact, the interview and any associated letters will be most effective in building your personal identity if integrated with a telephonic ploy such as "Your Name Is a Legend." Think of yourself as composing a symphony in a world in which there are few, if any, competing composers. A variety of contacts all playing on the theme that you are a real person, you are OK-different, and you are not being pushy about your qualifications should be your musical goal. Be creative and don't worry about your audience. It is more accustomed to listening to noise than music but it does, in fact, prefer music.

I won't bother you with advice about how to dress and act at these interviews. You have surely heard all that before. However, there is one thing that differs between these interviews with academic gatekeepers and others you may have had.

Any academician is, in the technical sense, a lousy interviewer but, that aside, it was you who asked to talk to him and not the other way around. Still, if you bombard him with carefully prepared questions he'll begin to feel like a victim of the inquisition or that you are improperly presuming an equality of status with him. However, exactly because most academicians are lousy interviewers, they will take over the conversation and permit you to avoid problems if you let them. Let them. You listen and nod your head.

So, all you'll need to have prepared is one question which asks your gatekeeper to "tell you about the graduate program," and one that asks him "about his own research." That's all he'll need for at least a solid hour of semimonologue.

However, if there happens to be any sort of research paper bearing your name as sole or co-author (even a duplicate of one already submitted will do), have a clean copy to hand him if he should run down. Simply say that the paper describes some work you've done but that you haven't decided (not: you are "unsure"; that sounds wishy-washy) whether to do more in this area. Of course, if it happens to be research in your gatekeeper's area, then you should express an intention to stay with it. Who can know one's own mind with utter certainty since Freud described all those unconscious mental processes?

The timing of your personal interview is — as was true of the "Satan Is Tempting Me" telephonic approach — of importance if it is to have the maximum benefit for you. Obviously, it is better that the interview occur before the dates during which your target departments are making initial decisions on applications. This implies that you should aim for somewhere in the last two weeks of February or the first week in March. If you cannot get away from home until after that period, a personal interview could still have a powerful effect on moving you to the top of a second round of applicants or moving you into that group from among applicants relegated to limbo. A personal interview in which you do little more than dress neatly, look serious, and agree with your gatekeeper is an absolute atomic bomb by comparison with other identity-building ploys. If you also speak clearly and to the point at hand, the interview will be of the power of a hydrogen bomb in establishing your identity.

Packaging Yourself

My advice here pertains to any situation in which you contact, by mail or in person, any potential gatekeeper. This includes your advisor, others at your home school whom you'll ask for reference letters and, certainly, anyone in your target departments.

My purpose is to warn you that first impressions are sometimes the last impression a gatekeeper will have of you before making some decision that will affect you in reaching your goals. So, it is in your own interests to present the first impression you actually prefer, rather than the one that just happens to be struck.

Any human being has many different faces — to a lover, to an authority, to an acquaintance — and each is as real as the other. Surely you have no obligation to be the person someone else wants you to be for his purposes when those purposes are not your own. Then, surely you should feel free to be the person you want to be for purposes that are your own. And, that's all that packaging yourself is about: being the person you want to be for your own purposes.

It's trite but true that outward and visible appearances have an enormous impact. A well-known social analyst, Niccolo Machiavelli, captured this idea when he said, "men in general judge more by the eye than the hand, as all can see but few can feel. Everyone sees what you seem to be, few experience what you really are" (from *The Prince*). Therefore, whenever you can be seen by a gatekeeper — whether in person or vicariously through something you have written — remember that his attitude will be more greatly affected by what is visible than you or he might imagine.

All home school contacts with gatekeepers will involve both your physical and written visibility as will some target school contacts. Some target school contacts will involve only written visibility. Therefore, I'll focus on written visibility here with the single general warning that you should look like a serious student whenever you are physically visible to a gatekeeper. If you'll practice nodding your head a lot, you won't have many problems with appearing to be a serious student when in contact with a gatekeeper. *He* will do the actual talking and probably remember you as well-spoken.

My most general advice about visible writing is that it should all be typewritten and in these days of correction tapes or ribbons there is no excuse for strikeovers. Also, as I've said several times elsewhere, you must spell and use words correctly.

For your home school gatekeepers, you will write such things as your curriculum vitae (CV, in *clubspeak*), lists of faculty at schools on your *preliminary lists*, and, perhaps, papers based on independent research or reading. These are described later.

At your target school(s), your visible writing will include the various parts of the application, letters you write in connection with a telephone or interview contact, and, again, any papers having to do with research you've done as an undergraduate.

Most of your compatriots-in-application will write no more than is directly requested on the application itself. Most of them will imagine that it is solely the content of what they write that makes any difference. Most of them will think they are preparing one application that will be sent to various schools. I am sure that they are mistaken in all these matters.

See My CV

This brief document will be of use to you at several times during your contacts with gatekeepers. You should always have a clean photocopy in your briefcase, folder, day pack, or whatever it is that students on your campus use to carry things in. You can never tell when, say, some home school gatekeeper whom you've asked for some kind of "guidance" will ask you about your academic history or plans. It will really impress him if you have this CV at hand.

I said this document should be brief. In fact, no more than one typed page is best. All you want to accomplish with it is to display your preparedness, your name, and some framework that may be used to identify you in memories, attitudes, or reference letters. I've composed a sample CV in a form suited to these purposes; it's in figure 1.

Figure 1

Curriculum Vitae

NAME: Sam Student

UNDERGRADUATE:	CURRENT MAILING ADDRESS:
University of Wow	4 Edgewood Road
North Medrow,	Medrow, Massachusetts
Massachusetts	09321
Major: Biology	TELEPHONE: (208) 472-6389
Minor: Biochemistry	(208) 471-9122

INTEREST AREAS: Marine studies, ecology, vertebrates, protein toxins.

PAST RESEARCH EXPERIENCE:
1. An independent research project on tidal pool ecology under the supervision of Dr. Henry Clam.
2. Acted as assistant in project venom of *Sea snakis* under the direction of Dr. John Bite.

PAPERS (copies available):
1. Snakes, snakes, and more snakes. Mimeo, 1980.
2. The probable effects of nuclear power plants on the water temperature in the local marine environment. Mimeo, 1979.

There are several things to notice about this sample CV. First, it lists several interest areas, both generally and specifically. People with several different sorts of interests will be seeing it. Why not include your interests within their interests? At least, why not mention some general area that is almost sure to cover their specific interest areas? Who knows? Maybe those will be your interests when you find out more about the field.

Second, this CV contains essential information only. It

does not list your past courses (or grades, certainly); that is what transcripts are for. It does not give details of your height, weight, and marital status. These are irrelevant.

Last, the CV stresses the research, writing, or artistic activities that are most related to the field in which you're applying.

Your gatekeepers will believe that they can tell most about what you will do from what you have done. Don't be concerned that the papers you list here are not works of Nobel Prize quality. In the first place, you'll probably never be asked by a gatekeeper to produce a copy. If you are asked, it will probably not be read carefully. Consequently, it is more important that it be typed neatly than anything else since almost none of your peers will have even prepared such papers to say nothing of informing gatekeepers of such research.

See My List

These lists will be of full professors in your target departments who are *maybe big names*. One of the listed departments (whether or not it's one of your targets) should be the alma mater of the home school gatekeeper to whom its shown (i.e., your *tipster,* advisor, or letter writer). Since there may be as many as four home school gatekeepers whom you contact, it follows that four lists, differing only in these four alma maters and their respective faculties of full professors (see figures 2a and 2b) may be required.

I have constructed two sample lists to illustrate the necessary information. Imagine that List A (figure 2a) would be shown to a home school gatekeeper who received his Ph.D. from Whoopie U. and List B (figure 2b) to one with his Ph.D. from Hello U.

Again, there are some key features to notice on these lists. First, each is arranged to fit on a single typewritten

Figure 2a
List A

Sam Student
Proposed graduate area: *Social Psychology*
Interests: Groups, conformity, consistency theory,
       and attraction.
Graduate Departments of Interest:

A. *Aardvark U:*
    Harold H. Smith
    David J. Myers
    Maxton K. Lynt
    Jean M. Lawson
    Norbert G. Fally

B. *Whoopie U:*
    Denton W. White
    Stanley T. Fall
    Harriet M. Jones
    Steven A. Miss
    Joan C. Gate
    George L. Famson
    Walter K. Davids

C. *Stave U:*
    Helen M. Donne
    Karl V. Hass
    Julian B. Fox
    Jerome R. Lult
    Martha L. Dace

D. *Heslip U:*
    Maxwell Zeiss
    Alvin T. Lake
    Robert R. Dent
    J. Donald Hipp
    Sarah Zame
    Donald P. Jackson

page. Second, the alma mater of the gatekeeper who is shown the list is treated as if it were one of your target departments. Of course, it may actually be one of them. Last, only minimum information is on the list. This is simply a list you expect to trigger your gatekeeper's commentary about the name status of the indicated faculty. Don't confuse the issue by giving your gatekeeper too much to process.

Your gatekeepers' alma maters can be discovered (a) on the *brag sheet* distributed by your home school department

Figure 2b
List B

Sam Student
Proposed graduate area: *Social Psychology*
Interests: Attitude formation, consistency theory,
          and attraction.
Graduate Departments of Interest:

A. *Aardvark U:*   B.   *Hello U:*
    Harold H. Smith   Eric L. Sullivan
    David J. Myers   Margaret B. Thompson
    Maxton K. Lynt   David Dash
    Jean M. Lawson   Marie A. Hall
    Norbert G. Fally   Jeffrey C. Masters
                                    Charles A. High

C. *Stave U:*   D.   *Heslip U:*
    Helen M. Donne   Maxwell Zeiss
    Karl V. Hass   Alvin T. Lake
    Julian B. Fox   Robert R. Dent
    Jerome R. Lult   J. Donald Hipp
    Martha L. Dace   Sarah Zame
                                    Donald P. Jackson

or (b) by consulting a directory published by your gate-keeper's national association.

If your home school grants a graduate degree in your gatekeeper's field, it is easiest to ask at the departmental office for any information sent to prospective graduate students. It will contain a *brag sheet.* If your home school doesn't grant a graduate degree in his field, the reference librarian will help you locate the appropriate national association directory. If those two sources fail you, try a casual conversation with your *tipster.* It's not classified information and most faculty know their colleagues' individual alma maters.

See My Papers

These papers, perhaps originating in independent research or readings courses, or, perhaps, merely bearing your name as a third author and written by someone else may cause favorable impressions in any number of ways.

First, it is probably worth your time to prepare them (or have them prepared) in ditto or mimeograph form. This, of course, suggests that many copies were needed originally for distribution to other interested parties. It also encourages you to clean up the mistakes in spelling or usage that may have been tolerable before but are no longer so.

Obviously, it would do no harm to prepare the copy in the format that is standard for journals in the field to which the paper pertains. Examine a few recent issues of those journals if the field is one that does not have a specific publication manual for use as a guide. If there is no such official guide, there are certainly enough manuals on how to write for publication available in the library that you'll have no trouble finding one.

Second, these papers can influence the creation of a favorable identity image if you send them separately from the standard application to individual gatekeepers in your target departments. You will not be thought pushy for doing this. Academicians do this to one another all the time. Just write a mild cover letter to the effect that you would like the enclosed paper to be added to your application folder. Be sure it's addressed directly to one of the gatekeepers in your target department, never to the graduate school and never to the department head or chairman. If you do those things, a secretary will merely open it and add it to your application folder. That would be a waste of the potential of your paper.

Last, if your paper is actually on some subject related to

the interests of a particular faculty gatekeeper (at home or away), you'll earn potential follower points directly. Think carefully, therefore, about whether there isn't some title for your paper that will catch the eye of a particular gatekeeper.

Furthermore, where is it written that slightly different versions of the same paper cannot have different titles? Nowhere, is where. Still, if such different versions should exist, it's not wise to send them to the same department. Remember Principle 1; it applies here.

I should also warn you that there are risks (controllable, I believe) in presenting a gatekeeper with a paper you've written. Even so, I am convinced that you will overestimate these risks unless you receive realistic advice from someone about them. Almost all students I've known— from *super* to *gamble*—overestimate these risks.

Assuming the copy is clean (with respect to typing, spelling, and so on), the biggest risk is that you may be writing about a subject in which your gatekeeper is (or, fancies himself as) an active researcher. Of course, he may not read your paper carefully but simply register that you have "promising interests." However, if he does read it you may be sure that if there are any of his own relevant publications that are not cited, he will notice that fact. The Rule of Inverse Impact applies here: the smaller his name, the larger the unfavorable effect of not citing his relevant publications.

Happily, there are very few papers you are likely to have written at any time that cannot be improved by including a few more citations. No text need be changed, mind you. Just a few judiciously chosen citations added at reasonable places in the existing text have been know to markedly improve many otherwise undistinguished student papers.

Closely related to "missing citations" is the prospect that

your gatekeeper will think the research you describe to have been misinterpreted. It will not trouble him that it has been badly conducted (if it has) — he assumes that it's always necessary to teach any new student how to do the scholarly work of his field. But, interpretation — that's another matter!

If your paper is some sort of review of what others have said and done, you needn't worry about being thought at fault for the interpretations you recount. If your paper is some sort of empirical research, it will probably have been reviewed by an instructor on whom you can put the responsibility for interpretations with a title page note expressing your "thanks to Professor Whammy for his advice on preparation of the manuscript in its present form." However, if your paper is some sort of essay, you are best advised to see that the views you express concur with those held by your various gatekeepers. If you'll recall, I told you earlier that a new manifesto would be judged by those reared under the old manifesto, and they would not relish being described as blind reactionaries.

I've said that most students overestimate the risks involved in showing their papers to their gatekeepers. They do so, I believe, because they underestimate the degree to which academicians hunger to create people like themselves. No matter what they may say, and no matter what their reasons may be, academicians yearn to transmit something of themselves to the future. In this regard, they differ little from other human beings.

Consequently, they will make allowances for the fact that you are a student. And, your papers, even though not the most brilliant imaginable, will be an indication that you have the promise of becoming the conduit to the future they need. You will be *OK-different* from other applicants. You will be noticed and you can prepare to have that notice be favorable. It is only your own preconceptions of "what might happen" that will prevent you from capitalizing on the way things are.

See My Future

It is a common part of graduate applications that you are asked to write a statement about your career plans and interests. I'll discuss this statement in more detail in Your Heart's Desire (chapter five). Suffice to say here that this statement, too, can and should be adjusted (within reason) to the sorts of interests you know your gatekeepers have from your knowledge of their publications. The general idea is to construct a different statement for each target department so that each will see clearly that you are exactly the sort of student they need.

FOUR
Taming the
Wild Reference

Generally speaking, letters of reference have no known validity as predictors of graduate school performance, success in the field, or anything else. They are not worthless *in principle*, I suppose. They could have predictive value. But, they don't—as far as any studies that I've seen show. The brute fact is, however, that academicians believe they contain predictive information and do pay attention to them. At least, academicians pay attention to *some* of them.

Your goals are to acquire letters of the sort that will be given attention and which say things about you that will aid your campaign. Most students do very little that is calculated to achieve these goals. This is partly understandable because they don't know the pressure points of their letter writers. It's partly understandable because they mistakenly believe that what will be in one of these letters is beyond their control. It's partly understandable because they mistakenly think a letter describes reality rather than that view of reality the writer has had the opportunity to see.

Students want "good" letters. They just don't know how to get them.

Some General Stalking Tips

Most departments will require three letters of reference. Unless you are specifically directed otherwise by a particular school, all of these letters should be written by an academician in the field in which you're applying.

If you're applying in geology, forget the psychology professor who knows you better than your mother. Geologists will give very little attention to a letter from a psychologist (or, other non-geologist).

Beyond this there are many inside tips on the general subject of reference letters it will benefit you to know. All of these apply with a vengence to dealing with any letter writer you'll approach in your home school so I'll cover them now.

Those Who Write Letters

Certain individuals will expect to write a letter for you. These people are your academic advisor and any who supervised you in some independent research or reading activity (either formally or informally). Students seem to believe that they are asking a special favor of these people when requesting a letter of reference. That is not true. It is commonplace as far as advisors or course instructors are concerned. None is likely to relish the task but all do expect to be asked to do it. Go ahead and ask — politely of course.

Application requirements differ among various graduate schools. Some will provide you with a form that you are to give to those you've listed as references. Some schools provide no form and the letter writer is left to his own devices.

Some who write letters for you will have a secretary type a ribbon copy on college or university letterhead that is either sent directly or photocopied to be sent to all schools for which you've requested a letter from the writer.

A ribbon copy sent "as is" is better from your point of view since it gives the appearance of greater personal interest in you than does a photocopy. Still, if you ask for letters to five schools all at the same time, a photocopy is probably the best you'll get. If your time schedule allows you to ask for each letter one at a time—as though you were making your decisions about where to apply one school at a time—you might increase the chances for five ribbon copies.

It's not of major importance, though, since recipient gatekeepers are well aware of the routine practice of typing one letter for subsequent photocopying. They know from personal experience how difficult it is to cope with the large number of requests for reference letters received by all academicians.

Some schools have systematized the "one letter" procedure by establishing a central file into which letter writers can put what they've written for various students. When you ask for a letter for a number of schools, these systems permit the letter writer to request a photocopy of your letter to be sent to the addresses you've provided. These letters have a tendency to bear the salutation "To whom it may concern" that undermines the impression you're trying to create of special interest in a particular department. Still, you may have little choice about it if such a system exists at your school.

Those for Whom Letters Are Written

It has become the practice, by reason of freedom-of-information laws and the like, to offer you the option of indicating whether or not you wish to surrender your prerogative to review the letters of reference that are written for you. Easily 75 percent of the students who have asked me for letters in the last few years have stipulated on some sort of form that they were reserving the right to examine the letters I wrote for them. I believe I know why students do this but, at the same time, I think they are quite mistaken in doing so.

I believe they do it with two sorts of wrongheaded ideas in mind. The first is that they think this "right to review" acts to minimize the number of unfavorable things I might say about them since, perhaps, I will worry about lawsuits and such. This is wrongheaded because it ignores the reality that if they think I know a number of unfavorable things about them, they should not have asked me for a letter and, anyway, I would almost surely not have agreed to write one. Perhaps there are academicians who take sadistic pleasure in enticing students into asking for a letter and, then, cut the suckers' throats, but I've never heard of one.

I've had students I've thought were seriously inadequate in either intellect or civilized behavior and some have even asked me for a letter. I have never written one yet even though, after trying to say no politely, I've been forced into telling the student bluntly that he wouldn't appreciate the letter I would write for him. In less extreme cases, I confess I've also taken refuge in writing utterly bland letters which were, nonetheless, unassailably factual. I am sure these did not help much but there was nothing unsupportable in them. All of the academicians with whom I've talked about this matter have done the same things. Who needs a letter like that?

The second wrongheaded idea here is that students ignore the fact that almost all of their letter writers were reared in days when such letters were held in the strictest confidence. Not only does the new openness offend some of the letter writers (there are not many human beings who truly welcome change), but students who reserve this right suggest thereby that they do not trust the letter writer. That is not the way to recruit anyone to one's cause.

Both these reasons aside, as a realist I'd just ask you to think about what good it will do you to reserve this right to review your letters. In fact, it is a right to review—*not preview*. You won't, usually, be able to see your letters before they go to the schools to which you've applied. You won't, then, be in a position to eliminate any letters you don't happen to like. Why, then, raise thoughts about your lack of trust toward your letter writers when it won't make any difference whether or not those letters are sent to your target departments. I see no point in it.

There are several ideal features that should characterize your reference letters. As an undergraduate, you'll not often manage to obtain such ideal letters but the more you can do to increase your chances of getting any of these features into your letters, the better for you.

First, the more "personalized" your letter the better. As you request a letter you should, of course, supply a copy of your CV (see Figure 1). This will give the letter writer some idea of your interests, graduate school plans, and most important, your past research experiences. Your fondest hope should be that some of this information will be worked into the letter that is written as though this was the personal knowledge of the letter writer. You can be sure that a letter saying little more than that you "were in" the writer's course in Mayan History and "received a grade of B" will not help you in any way except in meeting the requirement of having some number of reference letters. I'll return to ways of avoiding being *blanded* (see Glossary) shortly.

Second, any reference to your interests in the particular program being offered in a given target department will be

particularly helpful to you. Of course, your letter writer
will not know of this unless you tell him (and leave a typed
record that will jog his memory when writing time actually
comes). I've constructed a sample of such a document in
Figure 3. Just staple it to your CV and be sure your letter
writer knows what it is when you give it to him.

Figure 3
Tailored List

Sam Student
Graduate School Interests: Marine studies, ecology, verte-
                            brates, protein toxins.

Each of the departments listed is attractive to me for somewhat different reasons.

A. *Aardvark U:*
   Biology: Recent research
   on snakes
   Chemistry: Recent
   research on venoms of
   marine snakes.

B. *Whoopie U:*
   Biology: Recent research
   on marine iguanas.

C. *Stave U:*
   Biology: Recent research
   on ecological pollutants.

D. *Helslip U:*
   Biology: Recent research
   on marine vertebrates.
   Biochemistry: Recent
   research on protein
   structure.

This document may have the doubly beneficial effect of
inducing your letter writer to mention your interests in a
given department and getting you out of any informal
"one-letter" system that the letter writer uses on his own. A

target department gatekeeper who believes you have a special interest in some research in his department will take a second look at your application. The very fact that you know of this research will mark you as *OK-different*. You can, of course, get the information you need from the recent publications of those in the department in question.

Last, ideal letters will attest to your diligence as a student, your commitment to the field in question, and your maturity. You will have scored a number of points on these various dimensions by the simple reason of the signs of your planning. Your prepared CV, lists, and apparent knowledge of the general sort of scientific, scholarly, or artistic work represented in your target departments will override the effects of lowish grades.

In fact, your letter writers may never actually ask you about your GPA but will simply presume it must be a good one since you are so organized. And, even if they do ask, you can suggest that your GPA really doesn't represent your abilities fairly for special reasons. Your letter writers will buy that line readily in the face of the lists and such that you've prepared.

Those Who Receive Letters

These are the faculty gatekeepers in your target departments, of course, and from person to person the influence of reference letters will vary widely.

In the first place, most of them are accustomed to receiving letters that almost exclusively contain positive recommendations for admission of the applicant. They almost never receive a letter with a negative recommendation. I would estimate I have seen only three or four negative letters in over a dozen years. I touched on the reasons for this in the last section. The fact is that conceivably negative letters are filtered out of the system by actions of the applicants or the home school gatekeepers before they are ever written.

The standard or baseline against which your letters are implicitly compared is not, then, what you might naturally think it to be. You might suppose that your letters will be compared with letters about students receiving both positive and negative recommendations for admission. If that were so, any letter positively recommending your admission would give you an edge over all applicants who received negative recommendations. Since those negative letters just aren't in the sample typically received, though, the comparison is actually based upon the apparent enthusiasm in the writers' recommendations for acceptance.

This enthusiasm may range from zero (thereby *blanding* you) to levels limited only by the writer's active vocabulary of adjectives (thereby *beatifying* you; see Glossary). The applicants receiving the most common type of letter I've seen are closer to being *blanded* than *beatified*. But, then, they probably haven't had realistic advice.

You might think that under these circumstances, letters of recommendation would be given relatively little weight in the decision to accept an applicant. As I've said, this does vary but, incredibly enough, almost everyone gives more than zero weight to letters. Yet, zero weight is about what they deserve according to the available research information (e.g., Willingham, Warren. Predicting success in graduate education. *Science*, 1974, *183* (4122), 273-78). Still, those who will receive your letters won't behave as if that were so. They read them. And, they are influenced by them.

Needless to say (by now, I hope), they are more influenced by letters from (a) personal acquaintances, (b) *big names*, (c) *comer names*, and local *big frogs* — in that order. You are probably helpless to arrange for letters from the friends of your target department gatekeepers but the same is not true concerning the others. So, I'll turn now to the stalking of these other worthies by describing the hunt for *big names*. Exactly the same principles will apply to the stalk of *comer names* and local *big frogs* so I'll leave it to you to translate my advice to the sort of game available in your own home school.

Stalking the Big Name

It is possible that a *big name* may not be available to you in your home school department. If so, as a realist-in-training, you should aim at the biggest name around and plan to make up any points unavailable to you here with some artful dodging in other parts of your application.

If you don't already know the *big name(s)* in your home department the best working definition is also a simple one. Who is among the oldest faculty *and* has published many more articles, review chapters, or books than others in his age group in your department? After all, this is the way academicians judge *big name* status, so why shouldn't you? This is a working definition, however, and your candidate may actually turn out to be an ex-big name or, merely a *big frog*. Still, he's still likely to be the individual from whom you're best advised to seek a reference letter so what does that matter after all? If there is more than one such person, all the better.

Unless you happen to be in a *maximum class* department in which many are *big names*, two or three individuals at most will stand out above the rest in their age group and their publication records. How, then, are you to discover what you need to know about individual publication records? Age, I'll assume, is apparent to the eye.

Academicians live, are promoted, acquire tenure, get raises, and inspire *Festschrifts* (see Glossary) primarily on the basis of their publications. At least, this is true of academicians at any research-oriented university or college. All of these publications are carefully listed (and updated regularly) on each individual's curriculum vitae.

Recall the CV I earlier advised you to prepare about yourself and you'll have a rough idea of a *real* CV. Unlike yours, a *real* CV is better as it is longer and more precisely detailed. I have seen CV's of forty-year-old men and women that list each and every fellowship they received while in graduate school fifteen years earlier. You may be very sure that every publication will also be listed, along with honors, invited addresses, employment histories, and alma maters.

And those CVs for the older faculty in your home department are what you need. How to get them? Here are some ideas on the subject although you should, of course, adjust them to the local circumstances in your home school.

First, these CVs are not secret documents. They are documents of which the individuals whom they describe are proud, often overwhelmingly so. If your motives appear pure, then, you can simply ask the individual subject for a copy "so that you can read what he's written." There might be some paper you're writing for a course to which his work is relevant, or, your advisor may even have suggested that you read his work in connection with some conversation you've had. In fact, this can be a very effective beginning in the building of an identity image as an *OK-different* student. Keep in mind that when you express an interest in reading his work he'll be flattered, not suspicious. It might even be the first time he's been asked by an undergraduate.

Second, some departments maintain a file of current CVs. You might ask a secretary to give you copies of certain ones or allow you to pay for copying the CVs of professors X, Y, and Z. Again, perhaps there's a paper you're writing or some other reason for you to have a list of publications by each of these professors. Or, perhaps, you are merely seeking a few models so that you will be able to prepare a CV for yourself.

Third, though it's more work for you, you might search the index periodical in your field over, say, the last ten years. You already know the names of the older faculty in your home department so simply look them up, year by year, and keep score of the number of publications for each name. You won't miss any but those published in truly obscure or popular sources and those don't count anyway.

In case of ties or very small differences in numbers of publications, just plan to ask all of the professors for letters of reference. Even though you are usually asked for a minimum of three reference letters, you are not limited to that number. In fact, having five or six letters from people who sound as if they actually know you is a good way to suggest that you are *OK-different* from other undergraduates in your home department.

The *big names* you may locate are, as their colleagues in the shadows, accustomed to writing letters of recommendation. They are also accustomed to writing letters for students who are, in effect, total strangers to them. In fact, if they are *big names* they probably have had much less recent contact with undergraduates than their lesser colleagues and, consequently, encounter a relatively greater proportion of strangers asking for letters.

By reason of this, *big names* are generally more given than lesser names to the use of the noncommital phrase, the seems-to-be modifier, and the vague-trait description. These are all elements of *blanding*. For example: "Mr.

David Lost was in my introductory course. He seemed to be a good student. He tells me he is very interested in cryogenics. I recommend him for acceptance in your graduate program."

This letter reeks with *recspeak* (see Glossary) and every academician who reads it will know that. The use of the formal, honorific *Mr.* is not, by itself, *blanding*; however, since the writer did not later use the more familiar David (or Dave), *Mr.* is a sure sign of it. This, coupled with "seemed to be a good student" suggests that the writer actually has no relevant evidence to mention, and is a sure indication that no faintest memory exists of David Lost. One reads also a definite lack of enthusiasm into the "I recommend him for acceptance" in the absense of even a "strongly recommend" or "recommend him without reservation."

The letter is also too short. Letter writers who have even some small enthusiasm write at least two paragraphs. A second paragraph might have included some reference to personal conversations with Mr. Lost, or details of his interest in certain research areas, or that he has some clear commitment to graduate study. It would not, after all, have taken very much contact with the letter writer to provide him with some basis for saying these sorts of things. A *blanded* letter reveals that no such contact took place.

On the other hand, if a *big name* has written it, even a *blanded* letter is more likely to be noticed and provide some identity for Mr. Lost in the minds of the target department gatekeepers. At the same time, the worst you are risking in stalking a *big name* who does *bland* you is that the target school gatekeepers will decode his letter as one written out of duty.

You should also realize that any letter writer (including *big names*) does not have particularly high standards for saying some fairly positive things about you. This is undoubtedly one of the reasons that letters of recommendation don't predict much about success in graduate school. No one pays much attention to that fact, though, so that's not your problem.

When I say a *big name* hasn't high standards for writing positive letters I don't mean that you can expect him to fib on your behalf. He won't, if he thinks of what he's doing as a fib, that is. He might knowingly stretch the truth for one of his own Ph.D. students who is looking for a job but you are not of equal status.

Consider the situation in which he is placed. After he agrees to write a letter (and, with *big names*, your biggest problem may be finding him in town long enough to ask for one), you'll make moves that are virtually certain to mark you as *OK-different*. Moreover, he's not likely to be a mean person. Egotistical, probably, and tempermental if not handled properly, certainly, but not mean! Given that, he'll be on your side for a reason he does not even appreciate: he's writing a letter for you and almost all that he knows about you are the good things you want him to know.

The result will be that he will almost never write anything negative, will at least write something vaguely positive, and with some management will write as if he actually knows you. It is a no-lose situation for you. That he will know mostly what you want him to know follows from his status as a *big name* and that you are still an undergraduate. Several things are true of *big names*, although there are certainly well-known exceptions in some fields.

First, *big names* are busy people. That is, they are ordinarily inaccessible to undergraduates by reason of committees (of all descriptions), end-to-end trips to Washington,

D.C., where they tend their money trees (contacts in federal granting agencies), and invited addresses at universities across the land (northern in summer and southern in winter). In between the press of these duties they sandwich work with their own graduate students (i.e., "What have *we* done since I was last in town?") and conduct graduate or advanced undergraduate courses in their specialities.

Second, *big names* are so accustomed to being treated (which is not the same as actually regarded) as though they were nearly infallible, that they will follow their own opinions without doubt or deflection. If a *big name* believes that something is true, then as far as he is concerned it *is* true no matter what anyone else may believe. Happily, for you, this regularly includes beliefs about being a keen judge of a student's potential on the basis of a few unsystematic observations. Of course, the same is true in degrees among lesser names but let us not digress.

In that interest, you'll need two pieces of paper (both previously described): your CV and a *tailored list* (see Glossary) of target departments (see Figures 1 and 3). Armed with these weapons, and having memorized the title of your letter writer's most recent publication (having maybe even read it!), you're ready to approach. Remember, knowledge is power and you are better prepared than any undergraduate he is likely to have ever encountered.

First you may have to cope with the problem of managing to get into his presence somewhere. Don't be too particular about where "somewhere" is. If he is regularly not in his office he's probably promoted a hiding place somewhere on campus for use when he's in town. If you suspect this, lie in wait for him in the corridor at the conclusion of a scheduled class or, in the lobby of the office building at the time the faculty usually return from lunch. I don't think you should go so far as trying to trap him in a stall in the rest room, though. *That* would irritate him.

Openings

Here are some ideas to guide your opening remarks — after you have thanked him for taking the time to talk with you. Such thanks may work to make him feel a little guilty about being difficult to find. I believe guilt is a major motivation that drives most academicians and I'll say more about it shortly.

Suppose you know that he is the exceptional *big name* who does instruct a fairly large undergraduate class (seventy students or up). One surprisingly safe opening is: "You may not remember my name, Professor Cloudy. I was in your course on social movements. I'm Sam Student."

I said this was a safe opening because there is very little chance that he will recall whether or not you were in his course, let alone your name. It is an effective opening because you will also probably engage his feelings of guilt about "not getting to know" the students. However, the request you're about to make for a letter of reference will give him a means of reducing those guilt feelings by agreeing to do it and that will make both of you feel better.

Another opening of more general utility is: "I've been reading some of your papers on European cartography and my advisor suggested I ask you about related material. I'm Sam Student." If you use this opening you must be prepared for him to ask which of his papers you have read. It will be sufficient to have memorized two or three titles of the more recent papers. He will take it from there.

This opening may also be used if you are first approaching him to ask for his CV. If you're following my advice you should not, of course, ask for his CV and a letter of recommendation at the same meeting. Having *prior* access to the information on his CV will partly determine what goes on your own CV as well as what goes on the *tailored list* of target schools that you'll show him.

Still another tack that is extremely effective as an opening is: "I was reading your paper on the history of immigration and I noticed that you disagreed with Professor Dumer. I'm very interested in immigration and wondered if you have any papers in press in which you write more about your point of view on this."

This opening may strike you as requiring a sophisticated understanding of the field that is quite beyond your reach. Nothing could be further from the truth for one major reason. This reason is that there is seldom an academic paper published that does not contain some expression of disagreement with someone's prior work. All you need do is read the introduction or the conclusion sections of a paper to find the names of those with whom the author has disagreed, however slightly.

This regular reference to disagreements of various magnitudes follows, in part, from the nature of journal editorial policies in almost all fields. When a researcher or scholar has written a paper, it is submitted to a specific journal "for consideration." This means the receiving editor farms it out to a reviewer who reads it and recommends for or against publication in the journal.

Space in any noncommercial journal is limited. Many papers are submitted but relatively few are published. In psychology, for example, the main journals have had somewhere around an 80 percent rejection rate of submitted manuscripts for some years. This has many practical consequences but the most germane here is that authors strive to write their papers as if each has something different to say from previously published papers. And, as in the newspaper business, there is nothing newsworthy about agreement.

Snow in January in Minnesota is not news unless it is an enormous amount of snow. But in July, even the tiniest amount of snow would be headline news. Consequently, an author of an academic paper focuses on disagreements in findings and interpretations between his own work and that of others.

It may be an ideal in various academic fields that the point of research is to discover regularities but it is also necessary (as in: publish or perish) to accumulate *published* papers. Individual researchers are faced with either being realistic about this necessity or being punished by terminal appointments, no promotions, or no pay raises. It doesn't take much of a psychologist to understand why realism is the chosen path. In short, you won't have much trouble finding the names of people with whom your *big name* letter writer has disagreed. This information will be given prominent attention in his papers because he knows better than to allow a reviewer to miss the difference between his paper and prior papers.

There is another nice touch in this particular opening that will mark you as *OK-different*. This touch is in the use of the *clubspeak* hip phrase *in press*.

In fact, this phrase designates something that has been accepted for publication in a journal or book but has not yet been printed. You can always ask gatekeepers about things that are *in press* without undermining your image as one in the know. A paper, chapter, or book that is *in press* is usually known only by a very small number of people (the author and other specialists to whom he's sent copies) and it will not be expected that you should know of it.

And, since it has been accepted for publication it has already received the stamp of approval by reviewers and editors. It's the functional equivalent of something actually published. For your guidance and use, I've defined a number of clubspeak terms under the heading *papertalk* (see Glossary) that all relate to publications. You'll score points by working them into your conversations with gatekeepers. Virtually none of your undergraduate colleagues will ever have heard of most of them.

The Middle Game

After opening with some gambit that gets his attention either by arousing guilt or, preferably, his interest in his own interests, be prepared to follow his lead. If you use the guilt ploy I described, he'll probably say something about how large classes are becoming these days. This is the rationalization he has been using for years to account for having so little personal contact with undergraduate students. You should be quick to agree since this suggests you understand that none of the blame is to be placed on his head. After all, what could anyone do in the face of the number of students with which he has had to cope in recent years?

If you use either of the other two gambits—those that rationalize your meeting with him on the basis of your interest in his research, or writing work—be ready to take notes. I've already discussed this point in describing your first approach to your *tipster*; the same considerations apply.

He will go on for some time but watch carefully for signs that he's beginning to exhaust responses to the opening you put to him. You should guard against letting him go on without check. If you do, he will flit from subject to subject until so much time has been taken that you'll be pressed into hastily making your own pitch.

The idea is to switch him from his interests to yours without being too blunt about it. You must try to keep the total meeting time to the duration of twenty to thirty minutes at most unless it is utterly clear that he wants to chat on. And, even if he does seem to want it, it's better for you if most of that extended chat is about you and your plans for graduate school.

Sieze your opening then with some such remark as: "While I'm here, Professor Cloudy, I wonder if you'd mind looking at this list of departments that I'm considering for graduate work. I'd very much appreciate knowing what you think of them." As you say this, you should hand him your two prepared documents — your CV stapled on top of your *tailored list* that includes his alma mater. That's right. Just hand them to him. What's he going to do? He'll not only take them, he'll at least glance at your CV and then read the list of departments so that he can say something about them to you. What else can he do without being a rude slob about it? Moreover, while he's reading he'll have time to get over the shock of encountering an undergraduate student who is as organized as you are.

These two documents will give him food for another spell of monologue. Listen as though every word were a pearl. Also, take notes. If he asks you questions, keep your answers short and to the point. Avoid as the plague the use of filler sounds such as "uhh," "like," "y'know?" "right?" and "OK?" in your speech. You may use those sounds all of the time in your natural conversation, but, this is not a natural conversation. This is a performance, and the role you are playing is not one that calls for the type of speech that includes these filler sounds. At least, you may be sure that your audience-of-one will not be impressed favorably if it does include them. The principle here is the common one that we like best those who are similar to ourselves.

The End Game

As he begins to exhaust himself of the good advice he's been giving you about your *tailored list*, be alert for your chance to put him where you want him: writing a letter for you.

There are two different plans you might follow here. The first should be followed if you have had great difficulty finding your letter writer around the department long enough to get into his presence at all. This plan involves asking for your letters at this first meeting for the simple reason that you may never get another chance. If you think you will be able to see him a second time before he must write your letter, use the second plan. Still, don't count on a second appointment, however firmly he might make it. *Big names* are notoriously untrustworthy when it comes to keeping appointments. The same is true of all other academicians.

The first approach is to say something like: "I appreciate your advice, Professor Cloudy. Since all the graduate schools require recommendations from people in the field, would it be possible for me to list your name as a reference?"

Notice here that you don't actually utter the words "letter of recommendation." Your letter writer knows, of course, that listing him as a reference is almost always the same thing as asking him to write a letter, but there's no point in emphasizing that fact. And, more important, as long as you don't actually ask him to write a letter, he can still hope he'll only be required to fill in one of the "check list" forms that some graduate schools use in preference to a free-style letter.

If this is your first contact with him, he may very well try to put you off with some remark about not knowing you well. If he does you can almost surely scare him out of such a line by immediately suggesting that you meet with him again so that you can discuss your background with him in greater detail. The last thing he wants to do is take up his time talking about your background. Of course, if he is a rare full bird and does agree to your suggestion, try to set an appointment in the immediate future at a specific time, even though he is an odds-on bet to forget about it. Long shots do come in occasionally and, if he misses the appointment, you'll be in a position to play on his guilt about that while seeming to epitomize complete understanding of his busy schedule.

The minimum that the first plan requires is that he agree to be listed as a reference. After he has agreed to being listed as a reference, you can simply say that you'll leave a note with his secretary of the addresses to which you are asked to send references. Of course, it should be your intention to have as many additional brief contacts with your *big name* as you can manage given his on-campus schedule before you supply these addresses. There are out-of-channels contacts, faculty mailboxes, telephones, and, if you are fortunate, additional office visits that can all be used to build your identity in his mind before he writes.

The second approach is simply to thank him for his advice about readings and the graduate departments of interest to you and leave. You should not even hint about a letter of recommendation! You won't mention that subject until you have more than begun to build an identity in his mind. As in the first plan, there are out-of-channels contacts, faculty mailboxes, telephones, and additional visits to his office that should be explored with the purpose of becoming a real person to him. Then, after you have

become a familiar individual, it will be the most natural
thing in the world to ask him for permission to list him as a
reference.

The application information you'll receive will set out
various dates by which your credentials (including your letters) must be received by your target departments. In practice, it is often quite risky to be guided by these dates
because there is variation in actually observing these dates
among departments at even the same university. Your
tipster can help you on this subject since he will have some
idea of the de facto practices in your field no matter what
the published dates for the university might be.

I think here, for example, of the fact that the published
final date for submission of applications at my own university is June 1. Nevertheless, in the psychology department,
essentially all decisions about new graduate student admissions are complete by the end of March. What do you suppose happens to applications received in April or May?
Unless there is an unusual reason to call a particular application to the attention of some faculty member, nothing
happens to one received in these months. Such "late" applications are rejected as a bunch when a secretary finally
gets around to asking what to do with them.

I'll have more to say on block admissions and rolling admissions in the last chapter. My department employs a
block admission procedure for the coming fall semester. If
an application isn't in the "block" when the faculty meets
to decide on admissions, it's extremely unlikely that it will
receive any consideration. There are differences among
universities, fields, and departments in de facto dates as
well as practices for admitting students to the fall and
spring semesters. Your *tipster* can help you for your field.

All this relates to stalking your *big name* (or other)
references because you should take it as a fact of life that

they will postpone writing any reference letter until the last possible moment. And, often, well beyond that moment.

This means two things for you. First, you must begin stalking them as soon as you can collect the necessary inside information. You'll need time to stalk them properly as I've described it and you cannot count on them actually writing your letter when it will still do some good if you wait too long to trigger it.

Second — and this is particularly true when you face a block admissions system in your target departments — you must be able to give your references a deadline date that neither seems to crowd them nor is actually the date by which you must have your letters. Asking for a letter by "the end of this week" will be thought of as pushy by a letter writer. It might also suggest that you have not planned ahead enough to give them reasonable notice. I would recommend suggesting a date that is two to three weeks from the date you make your request as the one required by your target department. In my experience, this time period is sufficiently long for most academicians to imagine that they will "surely get to" anything by then.

Your actual deadline dates should be at least two to three weeks after the date you give your letter writer. If your application materials arrive early, there is no harm done. As I've said, they simply accumulate in a file until the faculty is ready to act on them. It is another matter for "late" materials.

Moreover, you should politely check with your letter writer about two days before the deadline you've given him to see if he's written your letter yet. The odds are that he will not have done so but, since you inquired, might now do so before the supposed deadline. Still, even if he doesn't manage that "deadline," you will have a two to three week cushion in which you can continue to inquire about a letter. A neatly typed note in his mailbox is perhaps the best means of making these inquiries following the passing of your supposed deadline. A note also gives you a chance to attach another copy of your CV. Who knows? He may have misplaced the copy you gave him earlier. And, if he didn't, what can it hurt if he has looked at your CV twice before he writes your letter.

You will almost surely think that what I've said here about "reminding" your letter writers to write will be thought pushy no matter how polite you are about it. If so, you are neglecting to consider two things.

First, your concern about having your letter written is entirely understandable to your *big name* (or other) reference. He expects to be asked to write such letters, remember? He may consider doing so a cross to be carried but he knows that you're asking because your target departments have required such letters from you. It's not your fault. It's their fault. They set the deadlines — not you!

Second, he has "freely" agreed to be a reference for you. And, having agreed, it is then on his back that the obligation to write a letter rests. He will generate his own guilt over the prospect of messing up your life by not doing what he said he would do.

There is no way that you could know it but academicians are marvelous at generating guilt for themselves. This is actually to say nothing other than that they are similar to most human beings. Understandably enough, though, academicians are particularly good at it since they live in a world in which there are no clear standards by which "enough" can be judged.

How many publications per year are "enough"? One more than the departmental average? One more than last year? There is no answer.

How many public honors are "enough"? Is one award for distinguished achievement by a national association and one prize for exceptional merit in research equal to one-half a Nobel Prize? Is a Nobel Prize "enough"? There is no answer.

How many research or study grants are "enough"? How many research assistants are "enough"? Again, there is no clear standard by which a measure can be taken.

The reason is simple enough. Academicians are not engaged in tasks that have an ending. The research, or writing, or artistic creation that they do or teach has no definable limit. Even a very specific research question or writing project or artistic work — while having a short-term goal that may be reached — is thought of as part of the individual's work that will simply continue. And, as to teaching, those who are taught this year will, of course, be replaced next year by others who are to be taught and they, in turn, by others.

I once had an experience that I'll describe to you because I believe it reveals something of an academician's attitude about *the life*. I was riding in a bus that was stopped by heavy traffic for twenty minutes or so. During those twenty minutes I watched two men lay out the dimensions of a short drainage ditch and begin to dig the ditch with hand spades. My thoughts were tinged with a little envy as I watched them and recalled a research problem I had been trying to solve for several days.

I found myself thinking (somewhat enviously) that it must be nice to know that one was digging a ten-foot ditch and that when ten feet had been dug that was the end of it. There it was, all marked out by stakes, and all that was needed to complete the job was to remove the earth to a prescribed depth.

Now, I believe I could no more dig ditches every day

than I could fly under my own power. But my thoughts about working at something that has a definite ending were tinged with envy, I believe, because that's so very different from the sort of work I do. And, since other academicians do the same sort of work I do, they, too, are continually beset with self-doubts about whether what they have done is "enough." And, usually, they think privately (I believe) that it is not. Hence, they all feel a trifle guilty about research undone, papers unwritten, lectures unrevised, books unread, and students untaught. No matter how much has been done. It's part of *the life*, which, happily for those of us who live it, has an incredible number of intellectual and occupational attractions that outweigh the discomfort of these chronic guilt feelings.

A Cautious Test

Perhaps it would be helpful to confront here something I've mentioned before but which you are very likely to worry about as you think about stalking your key references. You almost surely have thought something like: "I'd never get away with what he's advising me to do. My letter writers would see right through it. They'd *know* that I had planned it out."

It will do no good for me to simply say you are wrong. You are, but it's understandable that you won't believe you're wrong. Unless you believe it works, you won't try it and you'd never have an opportunity to find out that it will work. So, since seeing is believing, I'll tell you how to test what I've said in a situation that can do you no harm, no matter what happens. If it works as I've said it would there, you can use it where it does count. If it doesn't work as I've said it will, there will be no harm done to you.

First, pick the *smallest* name in your home school in the field in which you plan to apply. A brand-new assistant

professor or, even a lecturer who just received his own
Ph.D. last year will do. Then, stalk him exactly as I've said
you should stalk one of your key references. Since
whatever he says in a letter won't ordinarily carry much
weight in your target departments, even a strongly positive
recommendation from him won't help much. However, it
will be one letter beyond the minimum of three you'll probably be asked to submit. That might suggest that, unlike
most undergraduates, you are known to a bunch of faculty
in your home school.

If you want to be especially cautious about testing my
advice, stalk this small name but supply him with addresses
of departments to which you do not plan to apply. The
stalking practice will do you good and his letters will never
reach your actual target departments so nothing he says
can hurt you. Amusing, isn't it? A full-dress stalk resulting
in letters to some number of schools who will never hear
another word about you. But totally safe, you must agree.

Beyond using your own judgment to decide how a small
name has reacted to your test stalk, you may want to
follow up to be sure he does write your letters, just as you
should with other letter writers. However, it may be sufficient for you to discover that your small name does
not—as you might fear—cry "gotcha" during your test
stalk.

If you are concerned that these letters from nowhere
might lead to inquiries from their addressees, forget about
it. Each admissions season every graduate school and
graduate department receives scores of partially complete
application packets. There are many reasons that could be
imagined for this but that's not relevant here. The point is
that graduate schools and departments are accustomed to
receiving such "incomplete apps," most of which are never
completed at any later date. They are held in a file

somewhere for a year or so to await possible completion and then dumped. The misdirected letters you cause to issue from your small name in a test stalk will eventually meet the same fate, if you do choose this ultracautious approach I've described.

Stalking Any Reference

Almost everything that I've said about stalking *big names* is applicable everywhere except, perhaps, that *comer names* and *big frogs* are more likely to be in town on a regular basis. *Little names* are always in town with the possible exception of the one or two weeks in the year when their regional and national associations hold conventions. Your academic advisor may be a name of any of these various sizes so I cannot generalize about how often he is likely to be in town.

In fact, you would not be far wrong if you estimated the status of a name by the frequency with which an individual is *not* in town. The more frequently out of town (and not just at home tending his lawn), the greater the probable status in the eyes of his colleagues in the field.

Beyond that, if a name regularly makes trips out of the United States you can be sure that individual is worth cultivating as a reference. Of course, the cultivation is all the more difficult in the case of such globe trotters since you often can't get to them.

All in all, the chances are that you won't have direct access to information about the frequency with which a name is elsewhere. Still, when you get a copy of a name's CV, be sure to see if he has listed papers and, particularly, colloquia and invited addresses that he has given. Both colloquia and invited addresses indicate that others in the field have asked the name to come talk to them on his speciality and they don't do that unless they have heard of him and his work.

One fact that you as an undergraduate will not know is that academic departments everywhere file some sort of annual report with the dean or vice-president of the school or college in which they are administratively located. This report is supposed to describe what happened in a department during the calendar or fiscal year just past.

Some of the information that will be listed in a department's report are the various colloquium visits, honors, and other such *puff claims* (see Glossary) of each member of the faculty in the department. These annual reports, like CVs, are not secret documents. In fact, they may be even easier to get than CVs because, while departments may not collect CVs, they surely file annual reports. You can use the annual reports over several years to discover which faculty have been hard on the invited address or colloquium trail.

A mere paper given at some convention or another is not as telling since most such papers are usually submitted for inclusion in a convention paper session (not unlike journal articles). Convention program committees are not known for their high standards in deciding which of the many submitted papers are to be scheduled. It's easier for the committee to rent another room in the convention hotel and give almost everyone a chance to read the paper submitted. If there's no audience but those giving other papers in that room, that's not the program committee's fault.

Your academic advisor is the one individual who will feel a very definite obligation to write a letter for you. His opinions about you, of course, will carry greater weight to the extent that he is in your sub-area and his name status is higher. As his specialization is more distant from the one you plan, his letter may carry less weight even if he is truly a *big name* in his own sub-area.

Beyond planning to ask your advisor for a reference (and, of course, any available *big name* who is in or close to your field), choose your other references on the dual grounds of (a) prior contact with them, and (b) their recognition status in your field.

The ideal plan is to begin cultivating your potential references in your junior year but almost no one does that. Next best is to have arranged some instructional or research relation with these someday-references in the first semester (or, quarter) of your senior year. It won't do you as much good to have arranged for such a relation in the last semester (or, quarter) of your senior year. Any letters should have been mailed by the time you've had extensive contact with faculty at that late date. Still, it is not without use to make first contact with potential references about a final semester independent study course even if you are reading this book early in your senior year. This sort of contact provides a natural means for you to begin to build a personal identity during the discussions of a possible late senior-year instructional or research relation. This is not quite an out-of-channels contact but can be an extremely valuable one because, no matter what might happen in the later course, the reference letter has already been written. Plans are almost always more impressive than accomplishments.

Recognition status has been mentioned already in connection with *big names* and *big frogs*. If your undergraduate school is a university (i.e., grants Ph.D. degrees, for present purposes), the same thing determines the recognition status of *comer names* and *little names*: how many articles published in journals, how many chapters published in books edited by others, and how many books published.

The greater the combined total, in general, the higher the recognition status.

The index periodical will lead you to the journal articles in a great many fields. Don't overlook the cited references in these journal articles. Authors regularly cite their own prior work, both books and articles, and they tend to take a broad view of what is relevant.

For Undergraduates
In Non-Research Colleges

These words of advice are for those attending an undergraduate college at which research does not happen. There are, I know, colleges at which it does happen but a useful idea or two might be suggested by this advice even to students at such colleges.

These schools are likely to be more diligent in seeking to identify undergraduate students for future graduate work somewhere than are the universities. Having no graduate program themselves (or, perhaps, only a few masters' programs), the faculty in their departments want to see their students "go on." They, too, are academicians and, generally speaking, they were socialized in graduate departments that subscribed to the norms of Academia.

It is particularly important, then, to become involved in any courses that relate to research, since the faculty who instruct these courses are most likely to be promising references. They may not be known in your target departments because they haven't published much but *you* will be able to become well known to them as an individual with research interests. This can lead to long, glowing letters of recommendation about your research interests from them. Such letters may not have the impact of letters from *big names* but their very length and wealth of personal detail will help your cause.

If you'll recall, I've already described three methods by which you can create an image in connection with this sort of research course. The opportunity for discussing your plans to take such a course with a potential letter writer are, perhaps, even more open to you at a college than a university.

Perhaps because their own lives are less dependent on building a publication list themselves, faculty at so-called teaching colleges who do publish are more likely to reward the contribution of an undergraduate assistant with a junior authorship. For one thing, there are no graduate students around for competition.

If you've worked for or with some faculty member on his research, offer to search the literature for citations relevant to the work. Very few people enjoy searching the literature though it's not difficult to do. If he lets you do that he'll feel he "owes" you something and that's likely to be a junior co-authorship on the paper "in preparation" which you can cite in a letter to target school gatekeepers. For your information, a paper is "in preparation" from the time someone starts thinking about writing it to the typing of the final draft. Scads of papers never get to the final draft stage but that's not your problem.

Most academicians are inveterate name-droppers. The names they drop are the names of people whose work is famous, those of their teachers even if only semi-known, and the names of people at other institutions whom they've met at least once

A letter writer's recommendation will have substantial weight with his teachers (or, mentors, as the stuffier types call them) or his acquaintances. The myth seems to be that such letters will not deliberately exaggerate the known facts because, after all, the writer might later be called to task.

If you've had a chance to listen to a faculty member talk informally for so much as an hour in all, you've heard the names he likes to drop. Check out the institutions in which those names are located. If they could fit on your *preliminary list* put them on with the thought that your letters of recommendation might get a more careful reading from the writer's teacher or acquaintances.

If your writer's own graduate department will fit your needs, be sure you apply there. You can be sure your letter writer will be known (you hope favorably) where he received his own graduate degrees and his letter treated accordingly.

One word of caution is in order about name-droppers, though. You should not trust that the names they drop are as close to them as it might appear. You'll have to gauge your name-dropper. Some move from the briefest of introductions at an annual convention to first-name dropping for the rest of their lives. I've even known colleagues to drop the first names of people who were dead before the name-dropper was out of grammar school.

One sure sign of an untrustworthy name dropper is that he refers to someone by his first name alone whom no one present can possibly identify. Obviously, there are a lot of Henrys in the world. How are his listeners supposed to know that he's talking about Henry Kissinger? It might, after all, have been Henry VIII, but what the name dropper is really doing is waiting to be asked, "Henry who?"

The employment situation in your field may be in one of the swings that brings research-oriented new Ph.D.'s to teaching colleges as a way to earn a salary. While this in itself might make you pause to consider whether you want to get into this field, these young faculty often have surprisingly good contacts with gatekeepers at higher class universities. It is worth finding out whether any new faculty from research colleges or universities have arrived recently at your college. They may well be worth cultivating for a letter of recommendation.

FIVE
Your Heart's
Desire

This chapter will deal primarily with the parts of your *soft credentials* over which you have the most control. These parts include your choice of a preferred academic advisor (PAA), your autobiographical statement of interests and plans, and your application for financial support.

Preferred Academic Advisor

A great many graduate application forms permit you to state your preference (if any) for a particular academic advisor. Even if you are not asked for your preference on the form itself, you should make it clear in an attached letter (or, some other statement that'll become a part of your application) that you do have preferences.

Expressing this preference is an important way to bring your application to the attention of the PAA you name. In the beginning and long ago, I was astonished to discover

that in most applications I read this preference was nowhere indicated. I was astonished because it is very well
known that we all give near automatic attention to our own
names. Your faculty gatekeepers are no different. Our own
names are very special to us all.

But, which PAA should you name to extract the maximum benefit from the attention your application receives
by doing so?

The first point to consider is that a preferred advisor
may or may not turn out to be the advisor to whom you're
assigned for very long. Some departments nominally assign
all new graduate students to one person and then distribute
them among various faculty advisors after arrival. Some
departments haphazardly assign a portion of the new students to various faculty advisors. It is expected that students will shift advisors according to preferences of the
people concerned after a time.

Even in those systems that do assign new students to the
PAA named there is allowance for some shifting upon mu-
tual agreement after the student has learned the territory.
The point is that to name a PAA on your application
doesn't commit you to a marriage you might later regret.

Second, there's little benefit in requesting a *big name* as
your preferred advisor. They are named by almost all who
do name a PAA. It will be no big deal to them if you do so
as well. Moreover, asking for a *big name* does not carry the
simple message (Principle 5) that you are especially informed
about the particular department. Everyone in the field
probably knows that a given *big name* is in a certain
department and has been for a number of years.

It's another matter, by the way, if your *tipster* or some
other source has informed you that a particular *big name*
has recently moved to your target department. If you're
applying for the first or second year in which such a *big*

name will be in residence, it's a good idea to name him as a PAA. Not only does that suggest that you know the score, it also may gratify the *big name* to see evidence that the whole wide world (even an undergraduate) knows of his every move.

Third, while there's some benefit in asking that a *little name* be your PAA, I think you can do better. You may be sure, I believe, that if you do request a *little name* (particularly one with relatively high academic rank), that person will notice, read, and be very willing to find some basis on which to support your application in later discussions of new students. That's not a small benefit by any means and you could do worse.

My reasoning here is that a high-ranked *little name* will be extremely gratified by even this slight evidence that he's known outside his own institution. These poor dears ordinarily see very little sign of this because, of course, they aren't known. But, they'd like to think they are.

Beyond that, they've been around the department for long enough that – for reasons having nothing to do with their name status – they may have acquired enough influence to aid your cause if they try. There is the risk here, though, that such a *little name* may be so estranged from his colleagues that his support could do your cause harm. On balance, I believe this risk is small enough to accept if there is another reason for requesting a *little name* as a PAA. I'll discuss one such reason shortly.

By elimination, then, we come to *comer names* as the most promising candidates to name as your PAA. There are several reasons that may lead a *comer name* to take a special interest in applications that name him. Any one might be sufficient to get him on your side.

A *comer name* is on the way up in the academic business and, in empirical fields, by now you know that means publications. Who do you suppose actually does most of the labor leading to those publications? Graduate students do it—that's who! Even academicians in the nonempirical fields such as English, philosophy, and the fine arts need graduate students who assist in various ways to produce the work by which scholarly or artistic activity is judged. A *comer name*, in short, needs troops to do the work that will determine his progress toward *big-name* status. If you name him as a PAA, he will surely visualize a likely spear carrier in his army.

A *comer name* is also not likely to be unhappy if the more established faculty in his department see signs that he is known outside his present institution. Since everyone in his department or sub-area will read your application, if he is named as a PAA it will make him feel a small glow of pleasure. He'd never admit it, of course, but that's what he'll feel.

A *comer name* is likely to be just old enough to have broken away from the exact gospel of his teachers and young enough to be constructing his own gospel. Since gospels are, in part, more credible to the extent that more people accept them, a *comer name* is eager to recruit those who seem likely followers. An applicant who expresses preference for him as an advisor is surely a more promising adherent to his gospel than one who does not.

Consequently, when you're collecting publication information for spotting *big names* don't neglect to spot *comer names* in your target departments as well. You'll need this information to decide who to name as your PAA. As in all cases, the *comer names* you consider must be *in* the sub-area you've chosen (temporarily, at least) for graduate study.

I've another creative device you might consider in connection with naming a PAA. I'll begin by asking you where is it written that you can name only one PAA? The answer, as far as I've ever seen, is that it's not written anywhere!

It's true that the many application forms I've seen ask about a PAA (singular) and provide only a very small space in which to write a name. Still, nothing says you can't squeeze two names into that space, or, even, attach a letter in which you describe your reasons for having equal interest in two different PAAs.

Assuming that you only squeeze two names onto the application form itself, you've doubled the number of people who might give special notice to your application because they each see it bears a very familiar name.

I believe that an attached letter naming two (or more, but don't be ridiculous about it) PAAs is still more powerful because it gives you the chance to reveal your knowledge of the particular research they've published, and to repeat the message that your own interests are in this type of research. It's an extremely smooth way to emphasize that you're *OK-different,* serious, mature, and know the score in a particular department.

The only risk you'll run in naming, say, two PAAs is that they'll be two people identified with entirely different academic camps. This risk is small in the physical sciences but, in the social sciences, humanities, or arts it is definitely a factor to consider. To take psychology once again as an example, if you named a follower of Carl Rogers and one of the several sorts of neo-Freudians, you'd either puzzle or amuse a clinical psychologist in your target department. As it happens, Rogerians and neo-Freudians go together like oil and water. There's not necessarily any antagonism between them but they just don't mix. If you named two such as PAAs it would look very much as if you didn't know the score.

One key to deciding at a distance whether two people in

your target departments will mix as PAAs is, again, to be found in their publications. A rough rule-of-thumb is, simply, whether they publish in (or cite articles in) the same journal or journals. If they do, they'll almost surely mix as PAAs. If not, have a care, especially if both are fairly prolific publishers.

Another key is whether they refer to the same people in the articles they publish. You should not expect anything like complete overlap in their references but a few names of cited authors in common indicates they'll probably mix.

This information is most easily found in either the *Science Citation Index* or the *Social Science Citation Index*. Both of these indices print the references (with author, journal name, and issue) from each cited paper. Since your *comer names* are listed alphabetically, just check their citations and compare the references each included in their papers. There's nothing to it now that you know where to look.

This brings me back to one reason for listing a *little name* as a PAA. You know he'll pay attention but he's published so few papers that it's difficult to convincingly portray your active interest in research if you name him.

My advice is to list as your PAA at least one *little name* along with one prolific *comer name*. It's best, I think, to attach a letter in which you explain your general attraction to the *comer name's* research as well as your interest in some particular research your *little name* has published. This letter should describe these as dual interests but not say that you expect to pursue one *or* the other.

I think this approach will get maximum mileage from naming a PAA. It will also avoid the possibility of listing two *comer names* who are locked in mortal competition with one another for the single tenured position open in the department. That does happen, although much more so at private universities than public ones, and my recommendation would lead you to avoid entanglement in such a struggle.

Can a Nobel Prize Be Far Behind?

We now come to the heart of your *soft credentials*, the statement you prepare describing your interests and study plans. I believe that the majority of all graduate programs request such statements from their applicants. However, whether requested or not you should plan to prepare such a statement. It's one of your very best opportunities to manage the impression your target school gatekeepers will form. No one can stop you from submitting it even if it's not requested.

Some Horrible Examples

I've been collecting excerpts for a number of years from the autobiographical statements I've read in graduate applications. My purpose was to illustrate to my own students what they should avoid in their autobiographical statements. The examples I've shown below are not, excepting one, exact quotations from these excerpts but I think I've been rather successful in typifying them.

> My lack of the level of knowledge needed has been glaringly apparent at times, which encourages my goal of graduate concentration in the area.

The phrasing is awkward, the punctuation is incorrect, and the comment actively draws attention to the applicant's weakness. There are no "objectivity points" to be gained by writing about what's wrong with your record. If your gatekeepers can't or don't see such things for themselves, why should you increase the chances that they'll just accept your judgment that your record's weak? Focus on your own strengths.

> In corroboration with a fellow student, I completed a multidimensional scaling study which investigated Heider's levels of responsibility people use when making responsibility attributions.

One incorrect word (*corroboration* instead of *collaboration*) can create a very negative impression. Unless you're a social psychologist you wouldn't realize that this sentence contains a bunch of clubspeak words which suggest the writer knows the score. But, that one incorrect word jars this image, even if a gatekeeper wouldn't admit it really made much difference. Beyond that, as in the first example, this statement is awkwardly phrased.

Rewritten, it might read, "I have completed a multidimensional scaling study of the attribution of responsibility. I collaborated with another student in this investigation of Heider's conception of the levels of responsibility that people use when attributing responsibility to others." The rewrite sounds a trifle ponderous, perhaps, but that's academic style. More to the point, it uses words correctly while packing in all those clubspeak terms contained in the original.

> For as long as I can remember, I have approached my endeavors with an attitude of energetic enthusiasm tempered by a potent drive to achieve excellence. I began to develop this personal style early in life and applied it to school, where I excelled, to music, theatre, and writing, which were my favorite extracurricular activities, and to a variety of community, leadership, and service projects.

The "for as long as I can remember" theme is heavily overworked in autobiographical statements. Usually, to be sure, the idea is expressed that the applicant has wanted to be, say, an economist for all this time. Assuming an ordinary sort of memory span, this takes us back to age ten or so and, if nothing else, the faculty in an economics department may smile at the mental images that stimulates.

In the illustration I've given, the applicant merely claims to have "approached endeavors" in a certain saintlike fashion for the period of memory. This statement reeks of affectation and is in dead violation of Principle 3 which warns against endangering your credibility.

You should use *clubspeak* as much as possible so you can't really hope to write entirely in simple language. I don't recommend *clubspeak* because it is more precise or more meaningful than simple English. It is not. I advise you to use it because it is the language in which those who will read what you've written speak and, I would guess, often think. Your use of *clubspeak* is to reveal to whose readers that you speak their language, that you know the score, and that you are *OK-different*.

Beyond this, however, you can avoid sentences flooded with commas. You can break complex sentences into simple sentences. You can "approach this endeavor" by imagining that each adjective will cost you $50 as you try to write something which describes a mortal being.

The first exposure to Social Psychology research was an awakening; to see that there was a body of theoretical and empirical information on this topic led me to desire further contact with this area.

This illustration expresses another common, though mistaken, theme. Re-read it. Sounds positively sexual, doesn't it? Avoid that. It makes the writer sound naive or suggests that he supposes the readers will be naive enough to believe that this sort of ecstasy would be admitted by anyone of mature mind.

The punctuation and sentence structure is also rather silly. Perhaps the writer's state of ecstasy accounts for that.

> My GRE scores speak for themselves in the quantitative and advanced areas. I feel the 35th percentile verbal score is somewhat lacking in validity in my case. The low score reflects my lack of understanding of some of the larger words used in the GREs which I have never before encountered and which I do not see as a hindrance to my graduate studies.

This statement is at least thrice cursed. The GREQ and GREA scores, by implication only, were fairly high but should be explicitly cited if there's an explicit citation of the lower GREV score. That's curse number one. When you do mention a low score in order to provide an interpretation suggesting it doesn't show the real you, find a way to mention your high scores at the same time. Balance the lower score information with higher score information, if you must mention the lower scores at all.

The second curse here is the frank admission that the low score was due to a lack of understanding of "the larger words." Words are the tools of academicians. It would be a rare academician indeed who would admit without physical torture that he doesn't know the meaning of any but the rarest or most technical of "larger words." Such an admission would be akin to the confession of a barber that he's never figured out how to use scissors.

The last curse is that the applicant apparently believes that his lack of understanding of big words is a matter of very little importance. The final clause seems to imply that anyone can surely do just fine in graduate study without knowing the meaning of a bunch of big words. There are very few gatekeepers who would agree or be eager to become involved with a student having this lowbrow attitude.

As one last horrible example of self-defeating confession, the following is an exact quotation from an application submitted so long ago that even the writer has (or should have) forgotten it.

My interest in psychology developed in grammar school where I was chosen as a "class fool," for no particular reason, in the seventh and the eighth grade.

Even a two-time winner of some distinctions ought to keep that fact to himself.

It wouldn't be much of a gamble for me to bet you felt a twinge of anxiety as you read my critical remarks about these horrible examples. I once had the same feelings when I thought about writing anything. I don't have them any more, even though I still don't believe I write nearly as well as I'd like. As a realist, I just do the best I can and, when it really counts, I pull in my poetic horns and try to write as simply as I can manage. I've read enough manuals of style and essays on style to have concluded that there are nearly as many opinions on the subject as there are authors.

Take punctuation, for example, as something you probably remember "being taught" by various people in your high school days. As it happens, I was exposed to what I later discovered is called structural punctuation. I had no idea then that there was any alternative even though a good deal of what I was told was correct never made the slightest sense to me. Well, everyone learns to cope with arbitrary rules as they grow up in any society and I did the same thing with structural punctuation. Nonetheless, I do remember reading Gertrude Stein, who used perhaps a total of six commas in all of the thousands of sentences she wrote, and wondering how she got her work published before she became famous.

I discovered later there were alternatives to structural punctuation (marking the sentence where a grammarian says it should be marked according to a mess of rules that make sense to grammarians, if not human beings) quite by accident. This was long after some of my high school lessons had embedded themselves too deeply for me to realistically hope to free myself of them. I'm sure this is the reason I once felt so anxious about writing things. I knew those rules were there but I didn't know exactly when I might violate them. It's much the same reason that many people feel anxious about preparing their federal income tax report each year. They have the vague feeling that they're doing something that might be punished but they don't know quite what it is.

The main alternatives to structural punctuation are respiration punctuation and rhythm punctuation and, of the lot, I believe I ordinarily wind up using a combination of structural and respiration punctuation. Perhaps I would write better if I were more consistent but I just can't get some of those grammarian lessons out of my head so I live with that fact as well as I can.

However, in writing your statement you are best advised to use simple sentence structure, a minimum of punctuation, and to read what you've written several days after you've written it to see if it still makes sense.

A General View

This sort of statement is difficult to write without sounding like a fanatic, a bumpkin, or a twit. Now that I've agreed with you about that fact, let's turn to the problem of coping with reality. The reality is that you must or should write an autobiographical piece to include in your application.

Ordinarily an autobiography is a statement about the writer's life. You might, naturally enough, think it sensible to begin at the beginning and go forward to the present. However sensible that seems to you, don't do it!

These statements should focus exclusively on your immediately past academic activities (research or reading, in particular) and then on your interests (research, in particular) in the period of your graduate studies.

Let your gatekeepers assume what they will about your aspirations following graduate school. A one-line statement on the application itself can handle that part of your future. Simply write where requested that you're interested in a career "in research and teaching." Surely none of your gatekeepers—themselves pursuing careers in research and teaching—are likely to be offended by that plan.

Your statement should begin, then, with some description of what you've done as an undergraduate in the way of research or specialized reading. Don't overlook empirical work of any kind that you've done in connection with any course as long as it may have had some plausible role in leading you to want to study in the field to which you're applying.

For example, suppose you took a lab course in introductory chemistry and are applying in geology. It would be reasonable enough to say that you learned in your lab course that you enjoyed systematically working through a problem. You might then say this led you to believe that learning to do systematic research in geology is one of your goals in graduate school.

This phrase—systematic research—may be used to describe your goals in any field of academic study. Every academician believes that his own research, at least, is systematic. You won't be commiting yourself to any particular type of research by writing about *systematic research*. This phrase functions much as does an ink blot. Each person who sees it probably will read his own meaning into your words without knowing it. And, it really sounds as if you're saying something quite specific. That, too, is important.

Obviously, if you have been associated in any way with any kind of research project, you should say so. It's not advisable to describe your role as one which could have been performed by any warm body. Even though you did nothing other than make photocopies of anything handed you by a graduate research assistant — you helped. Anyone who helps may also be said to assist. Anyone who assists is an assistant. The term *assistant* sounds somewhat more vital than the term *photocopier*. Sound as vital as you can without telling an outright lie. I do not advise lying.

Any sort of specialized or advanced reading you have done, on your own or in connection with one of those term papers you wrote, should be mentioned. Again, the role of this reading in affecting your reasons for the graduate study you plan is the feature to emphasize.

If you haven't done any such reading, perhaps you should take time to sample an advanced book or two before you write. Needless to say, you should definitely do this if one of your target school gatekeepers has written such a book.

If you have a paper you've authored (or co-authored), by all means mention the title(s) here. Also, include a one or two sentence abstract of the paper (or papers). An abstract such as this should be written in the most general terms and loaded with clubspeak.

Even if you do plan to attach a copy with your application, work the title and abstract into your statement. If you

don't want to actually show anyone a copy for some
reason, just say that copies are available. No one is likely
to ask you for a copy (unless you're applying in English).

I know I said there were *no* validity checks on your *soft
credentials*. If it weren't for English departments often requiring a sample of their applicants' written work, that
statement would be true without qualification for papers
you've written.

As to your immediate past, then, you'll describe any
relevant (a word which has only the limits you impose)
research, course, and reading experiences. Do not clutter
up your statement with descriptions of your nonacademic
activities. As I've said before, gatekeepers just aren't interested in the club officerships you've held, your hobbies,
or your civic activities. When you include this sort of thing
one result is to increase the length of your statement
needlessly.

These statements should be no longer than two typewritten pages (single spaced) at the very most. If they are
longer than this they probably won't be read carefully.
Keep in mind that yours is not the only application your
gatekeepers will be reading. A long, long autobiographical
statement is very likely to receive a short, short skim.

Your interests in graduate study in your particular field
should appear to grow out of the research, reading, or
course experiences you had as an undergraduate. It's bad
form to say that you want to study engineering because
you've heard you can make a pretty good living as an
engineer. Similarly, it's thought rather immature if you say
you want to be a linguist because your father, or aunt, or
some family friend is a linguist. You'd think that this
would seem a perfectly understandable reason, but few
acadeicians see it that way.

Describing the manner in which your graduate study interests "grow out of" your prior experiences is particularly difficult to carry off smoothly. If you'll refer to the horrible examples I gave earlier, you'll see that none of them handle this *transition problem* (see Glossary) at all well. The approach I advise is through the human weakness of your gatekeepers: their own interests in their own research.

Each of your target departments will have one to five faculty members who are either in or very close to the sub-area in which you want to do your graduate study. You can learn a great deal about these people through your knowledge of their publications and the contents of one or two papers (the more recent, the better) that each has written. If you've located a biographical blurb on each one in a professional or commercial directory, you know still more about them. The *brag sheets* in which your target departments have described their faculty is another source of knowledge about the individuals of particular interest to you. Your *tipster* will be another source of information about some of these specialists.

In sum, you can easily get as much information as you need to know — at a general level — about the research interests of your particular gatekeepers. With more effort you can get very detailed information about their research interests, but you do not really require it to write your statement of your graduate study interests.

Your gatekeepers are wearily accustomed to reading statements describing interests that were obviously those of the applicant's undergraduate teachers. That's quite understandable when you think about it. Those teachers are probably the only living members of the academic specialty the applicants have ever known. Naturally enough, undergraduates are likely to suppose that all specialists in the field are more or less like their undergraduate teachers — right down to their research interests. It's also possible that having acquired some knowledge of what is done by his undergraduate teachers, an applicant feels somewhat more confident in writing as if that is something he wants to do.

Last, almost all undergraduates have the understandably mistaken idea that graduate school is like undergraduate school in that they may study anything within the domain of the field. From this, they conclude that if they want to be, say, sociologists, it's just a matter of getting into a department offering a graduate degree in sociology. Once there, they presume, there'll be courses in any sub-area of sociology that's around, they'll take those courses, write something called a thesis (sort of a long term paper, they often believe), and get a Ph.D. degree.

It's not so, I'm afraid, but if that's what applicants believe, then saying they want to study what their under-graduate teachers study is understandable. They think they'll be able to do that wherever they go. Consequently, if your statement is written to suit the interests of your target department gatekeepers, you will stand out as *OK-different* by contrast.

This is not meaningless posturing, by the way. Graduate study is not like undergraduate study. You will, in graduate school, either study one of the specialities of one or more members of the faculty as you find them, or leave. It is virtually certain that the faculty will not change what they do or teach because you want to study something else. Departments do vary considerably in the number of sub-areas of the field that are "covered" but only in giant departments could you hope for anything approaching complete coverage of a field in depth. Even then, it wouldn't mean a great deal to you once you'd settled into study in one of those sub-areas.

Only if you know there are faculty in your target department with research interests similar to those of your undergraduate teachers should you emphasize your intention to continue along that line. As a matter of fact, if this is true, your problem of describing the transition from undergraduate past to graduate future is virtually solved. Nothing makes more sense to an academician than that an undergraduate who has been shown the true path should want to continue along it.

Here is a point at which you'll find the publication information you've collected on your home department faculty of great value. Compare your home school faculty member's research interests with those of your target department gatekeepers. If you find a match — even if with the interests of the most junior member of your *home* school faculty — your transition problem is solved. Your graduate school plans can now flow very smoothly out of your undergraduate school interests in the research of this home school faculty member.

Even if your home school faculty members have never published anything relating to your target school gatekeepers' interests, they do teach courses that touch on different sub-areas in the field. If a target school gatekeeper has research interests in one of those sub-areas, you can manage your transition problem by referring to your initial interest in the related course lectures.

Having described your general and more specialized interests in graduate study in the field arising from your undergraduate experiences, you should then tailor your graduate school plans to the research interests of the gatekeepers to be found in each of your target departments.

A Fine Tune

I've already warned you that if you follow all of my advice you'll need to prepare a somewhat different autobiographical statement for each of the target departments to which you apply.

Some of those differences will enter as you deal with the transition problem I discussed in the preceding section. Even more will enter as you describe why you want to study in each particular target department.

You do not want to suggest that you're uninterested in the work of all but one of your target school gatekeepers. There's no point in offending those who aren't mentioned.

As a prospective graduate student, you won't be expected to have precisely specialized interests. Indeed, it's probably better for you not to sound as if you have completely closed your mind to anything but one particular line or style of research. Your prospective graduate school teachers will believe you don't know enough about the territory to be entitled to such a firm opinion. They'll expect to tell you what's what in the field and they won't relish your trying to tell them.

So, what to do? I think it best that you build your description of your graduate study interests primarily around the interests of the one or two target gatekeepers who are closest to what you now think are your interests. You may change, of course, but that's been said before.

However, your description should not entirely neglect your apparent interests in the work of other target school gatekeepers who are in or close to the sub-area in which you're applying. Here's one simple way to manage these two things at the same time.

I'm particularly interested in Dr. Peekers's work on Austrian history. His monograph on the Austrian Steamship and his other papers on inland water transportation, along with those of Drs. Sears, Montgomery, and Marris on aspects of European history convinced me that I wanted to do my graduate study at the University of Zigazag.

Notice Dr. Peeker comes first and reference is made to several of his publications. True, these are very general references but they are sufficient to make clear that something is known of their contents. You can get that much information from the titles of these papers alone. Then, the glory is spread around by mention of the other three Europeanists in this particular department of history. The phrase "aspects of" is a perfectly marvelous one for making a general reference without committing yourself to anything. Academicians use it all the time. Having opened on this note of general admiration of a number of people in a particular target department, turn your attention to one (or two) gatekeeper(s) in slightly greater detail. You can do this with the greatest positive effect by writing about one or two of their papers in terms laden with clubspeak.

Here are some things not to do when you write:

— do not include the complete citation of any paper you mention. The gatekeeper who wrote the paper knows it already and it would look as if you're being a bit too careful to parade your homework. Refer to a paper by a keyword in its title along with a clubspeak abbreviation of the title of the journal or series in which it appeared. Each field has its own clubspeak manner of referring to its primary journals. Use it if you know it but in slightly dressed-up form. This is a formal statement you're writing. If "Chem Rev" is the clubspeak term for the *Journal of Chemical Reviews,* then refer to it as *Chemical Reviews* or, even, *Chem Reviews.* I cannot guide you here but your *tipster* or advisor himself will almost surely use common clubspeak titles whenever he refers to journals in your field.

— do not suggest that you have a better way of doing anything. I hope that you do (or will have) a better way but since you're discussing your interests in your gatekeeper's research this is no time to express doubt about his way.

— do not dwell on the details of his publications you choose to mention. Your purpose should be to make clear that you're interested in learning more about some sort of academic activity and not in the minutia of one or two papers. Your most useful information for this purpose will come from the introductory and conclusion sections of a journal paper or, perhaps, from the preface of a book written by your gatekeeper.

— do not quote from the papers or books you are mentioning. Again, that looks as if you're working too hard at impressing the reader.

This is most certainly the place to mention any specialized skills you have that might be useful to the gatekeepers whose research has so attracted you. These could be almost anything, depending on your area. If you know anything about computers that would make you attractive in many fields. In some fields, speaking or reading a foreign language could be usefully mentioned. In some, any background in statistics is worth working into your statement as you refer to your gatekeeper's research.

Think primarily of skills that might be of use to your gatekeeper and not skills that you suppose will one day be of use to you in the field. I've already told you that it's graduate students who actually do a good deal of the labor associated with faculty research. That's why your potential use to your gatekeeper in his research is the thing to stress.

When you've come to the end of this description of your interests in your gatekeepers' research — stop. Do not search for a ringing final paragraph. Just stop. I have seen the sentence, "And, that's why I want to do my graduate work in your department" far, far too often. When you've finished your statement, stop writing and leave the trite tag-lines to others.

Each of your actual target departments should receive the message from your application that you're tuned to the local music. The part of your autobiographical statement dealing with your immediate past might even be common to all your applications.

You should deal with your transition problem for each department in a tailored manner. Describe how those undergraduate experiences led you to be interested in not only the area but the particular sub-areas of interest to those in each department. And, finally, let them know that you know about some of the details of what's happening in a particular department. It would also be very nice if you have skills that just happen to fit into what's happening. They will love you for it.

The Real Ins-and-Outs of Stipends

At last we come to money. Money that will be paid you for services rendered as an assistant of some sort, money that will be given you for scholarship or poverty, and money that you will be allowed to borrow for repayment at miniscule interest rates. There are probably more misconceptions about graduate school money matters among undergraduates than any other topic.

Such misconceptions are quite understandable since there are few sources of realistic information on the subject. I myself once decided not to attend a particular graduate school because the assistantship I was offered for the first year was described as contingent in later years on "departmental needs." What, I wondered, would I do if they cut me off in the second year for something over which I would have no control? I scratched them off for this reason alone.

What I've learned since then is that at almost all universities a graduate student must either flunk out or drop out to lose a stipend. Once you've been awarded money of any kind in your first year, only a financial disaster which is visited upon your entire department or program will result in even a reduction of the amount you receive in later years.

You might not get more money in your second or later years but that's something else. Almost all academicians are utter softies when it comes to taking money away from anyone for any reason except when their authority to award it has been taken away from them.

Financial awards and acceptance to graduate school are often theoretically based on independent decisions about each student. The practical fact is very, very different in all cases of which I've ever heard. If a department really wants you, it will be assumed that you must be offered something in financial aid or you'll go to another school which does offer money.

Even though there has been a fierce money squeeze resulting from the Feds' reduction of direct and indirect support of graduate students since 1971, your present-day gatekeepers were themselves socialized during the sixties when money was everywhere. In those days it was nearly mandatory to offer money to get the students who were wanted. Most academicians think that is still true. Whether it is or not is hardly your problem though the result is that departments do scratch hard to find money to offer both new and old students.

Since the scratching is sometimes very hard indeed, even *maximum class* departments are becoming cautious about firmly committing a "piece" of financial support to a student who may decide to go elsewhere. Even big sharks have competition from other big sharks. The same is even more true of *middle, lower,* and *no class* departments. As this class ladder is descended, there are more alternatives for applicants and there is less available money to award. Moreover, it is decreasingly likely that applicants will come to one of these departments unless offered aid.

Since the offer of financial aid may be an important part of the reason a student decides to accept an acceptance, every department is caught in a bind. If aid is offered one applicant who doesn't come, it may have been tied up too long to switch to another applicant who might have come if aid had been offered him. Still, there is aid to be offered but there's not enough to offer it to everyone. You can see why I called it a bind.

More and more departments are trying to cope with this bind by sounding out desired students by telephone. Some faculty member will call an applicant and tactfully try to discover if the student has already decided to go elsewhere. If he admits to this, the faculty member will probably not debate the decision but will surely count it fortunate that a firm money offer wasn't made.

This is the reason I warned you to be sure your application bears all possible current phone numbers. If you're to get into a conversation such as this at all, you must list a telephone number where you can be reached or, at least, where a message can be left for you.

If the applicant waffles (i.e., says he hasn't made a final decision), the faculty member will probe to discover if his own department is still being considered. If so, the caller will describe informally the financial aid to be offered if the applicant did decide to come. Almost all departments will consider this *if offer* (see Glossary) to be one that can be unilaterally switched to another applicant unless a definite agreement about a "thinking period" is reached on the spot. The applicant will want this period to be as long as possible and the caller will want it as short as possible. This time period is negotiable. If the depatment has gone this far, the applicant is definitely on their accept-with-money list. It's not too much to ask for a week of thinking time.

In this situation, never suggest you're waiting for another offer to come in. That might be enough to get you off their accept-with-money list. Unless this is the school of your dreams, it's safe to say you have already received another offer and you'd like some time to decide. In this case, your caller can imagine that it was his department from which you have been awaiting a response. If it is the school of your dreams, say yes quickly.

Never try to bargain for more money at this point (if you think the amount is too little). You can do that about three days into your thinking period when you call back to discuss your great interest in the department and your concern that you might not be able to stay alive on the amount of money they've offered. The reality about stipends is that there is usually a loose chip or two floating around that some gentle bargaining might bring to you. And, even if there's no loose chip at the moment, there's likely to be one come free sometime before you actually arrive.

Another student may change his mind after accepting an offer. This is considered extremely bad form but there's not much anyone can actually do about it when it happens. If your previous bargaining has been polite and plausible, such a chip might fall to you since it would be too late to use it in recruiting another new student.

Another reason that a chip or two may be available later has to do with the difference in times of the typical fiscal year and the applicant recruitment period. Most universities operate on a fiscal year that runs from July 1 in one calendar year to June 30 in the next calendar year. The most common recruitment period is, however, in the early months of the calendar year in which students are applying for entrance.

So, when a department is contacting applicants in March (for its September admissions), it may not yet know exactly how many teaching assistantships, for example, the central administration is going to assign them after the school budget is partitioned following the start of the next fiscal year (July 1). Each department will have been given an approximate number by the dean or vice-president who does that sort of thing but, since it's an educated guess, this number may be conservatively underestimated by one or two teaching assistantships. Or, if there should be an unanticipated undergraduate enrollment bulge in a certain department, the dean or VP may be cajoled into increasing the assignment of teaching assistantships to that department after he has seen the breakdown of the school budget in August.

It sounds utterly mad in these days of computers to say that individual departments often do not know their exact budget months in advance of each September. Mad it may be but it's also quite common.

All this can affect new graduate students even though it's not common for them to be assigned a teaching assistantship in their first semester. The effect is that if any additional teaching assistantships are assigned to a department in July or later, these will be given to old graduate students for whom *other* aid may have been previously scheduled; this other aid is then shifted to the new graduate students who have already accepted. It's an annual juggling act at universities across the land.

I hate to keep repeating it but you should keep in mind that departments must have new graduate students. If they've called you, your name is on a fairly small list of applicants they've decided to try to get. This doesn't give you a great deal of power but it does give you some. At this stage, they are not trying to keep you out, they are trying to get you to come along. They'll keep trying within limits and that's what gives you the power you do have. Still, you don't actually have your Nobel Prize yet so don't talk as if you do.

As a realist, I'm somewhat reluctant to mention this next point since it deals with a "rule" which is probably honored more by accident than by design.

Years ago the Council of Graduate Schools adopted a resolution to which all schools would be delighted if students conformed. This resolution reads:

> In every case in which a graduate scholarship, fellowship, traineeship, or graduate assistantship for the next academic year is offered to an actual or prospective graduate student, the student, if he indicates his acceptance before April 15, will have complete freedom through April 15 to submit in writing a resignation of his appointment in order to accept another scholarship, fellowship, traineeship, or graduate assistantship. However, an acceptance given or left in force after April 15 commits him not to accept another appointment without first obtaining formal release for the purpose.
>
> It is further agreed by the institutions and organizations subscribing to the above Resolution that a copy of this Resolution should accompany every scholar

ship, fellowship, traineeship, and assistantship offer
sent to a first-year graduate student before April 15.

My reluctance in mentioning this Resolution is due to
two things. First, there is absolutely no sanction of which I
have ever heard that has been applied to any student who
has unilaterally changed his mind after April 15. And, I've
known of a number of students who have done exactly that,
often without troubling to inform the school to which
they'd made the earlier commitment.

My advice is to take the best offer you think you're going
to get. Then, if an unexpected but more desirable offer
comes to you at any time before you're registered, take it. I
do think it would be civilized if you sent a note to the
school from which you've accepted an offer, simply telling
them—not asking their permission—that your plans have
changed and you will not be coming after all. Don't rub it
in by telling them you're going to another school; just say
you're not coming to their school (so they can do something with the free chip of financial support before it's lost
to the dean's contingency slush fund).

Second, this Resolution is worded to imply that you can
expect to receive a firm offer in the mail about prospective
financial aid before you've agreed to come. This is not generally true as I've already told you. Tentative offers made
by telephone are the rule today.

Some departments will send a letter to inform you that
you've been accepted to graduate school but that letter is
very unlikely to contain a firm commitment about money.
There may be some talk about it being too early to know
exactly what aid will be available for students. Unless they
specify a dollar figure of an offer to you specifically, don't
think about spending it.

These acceptance-with-vague-money-talk letters may be trying to (a) get you to come without money, (b) keep you from accepting another offer until they've heard from their first-round choices, or (c) tell you the literal truth. There's no reason why you can't call the person who signed the letter and discuss it with him. You may learn nothing more than you already know but it's a natural opening for a little identity-building. You might discover that he'll tell you much more over the telephone than he'd commit to writing. You have nothing whatever to lose and there's a good deal you might gain.

As a general rule, call anyone in your target department who sends you any kind of letter. Things happen very rapidly over a short time during recruitment season and you can use these calls to keep your identity alive in faculty minds. All you need ask is whether there has been any new development since you received the letter you were sent.

Stipends Galore

There are a bewildering variety of types of stipends (singly or in combination) available to graduate students at different universities. A few are awarded exclusively for financial need, a very few are awarded exclusively for academic merit, and most are awarded for some mixture of financial need and academic merit. Some stipends require performing some service connected with the undergraduate teaching program of the department, some require service connected with the research work of a particular faculty member, and some involve no service duties at all. Some forms of financial support are grants of authority to borrow money at low interest rates from the university or local banks that are to be repaid after graduation. Some forms of support are waivers of tuition fees, or general fees, or both. Others apply to the academic year and some to the summer period. No wonder applicants are confused by this crazy quilt of stipends!

You'll find the basic descriptions of the stipends I'll mention in the financial-aid guides to which I directed you at the end of chapter 2. What I want to do here is tell you about the differences among them that mean something to a realist.

Teaching Assistantship

This is probably the most common form of graduate stipend. It may have different names at different universities but it boils down to payment for services as a helper in undergraduate courses in the department. In theory, part of the stipend is for the academic merit of the student but part must also be earned by doing a certain amount of work each week.

This work ranges from proctoring undergraduate examinations to leading weekly discussion groups (or laboratory classes) as a sort of programmed teacher who follows the schedule laid out by the faculty member in charge of the course.

There are many different sorts of work to be found in this range but most of it is simply work that must be done by someone if the undergraduate courses are to be conducted in the traditional way. Generally speaking, it is uninteresting work. And, anyone can do most of it the first time about as well as the thousandth time.

Still, there are advantages in being a TA (pronounced TEE A, if they called it something else at your school). For one thing, the stipend usually rises each year as you progress through graduate school. For another, some schools either charge lower tuition fees or waive them altogether for TAs. For still another, if your assignment is rotated among several faculty members over the years, you can become an identifiable person to other than your immediate advisors. It might be these new faculty acquaintances who will each year decide on stipend assignments for both new and old graduate students in the coming year. The same principles of impression management apply to getting along in graduate school as to getting into graduate school.

Most faculty are reluctant to offer a new graduate student a TAship. They want to wait a bit to see if that person turns out to have three heads (or, none at all). If you're offered a TAship, don't let concern over whether you're ready to do things on your own stand in the way of accepting. You won't do anything on your own until you've been there a while. Even then you won't do very much on your own.

It's usual for a TA to be assigned to whatever work that TAs do without regard to the student's sub-area of study. In short, a TA is usually at the disposal of the department even though a particular sub-area may have been authorized to offer this stipend to one of its own students.

In psychology, for example, most TAs are assigned to work in connection with the introductory course (which ordinarily has the largest enrollment) no matter what sub-area of psychology they may be studying.

Research Assistantship

This form of stipend is rarely offered to a new graduate student. If it is offered you and everything else suits you, take it. The work done by an RA is likely to be the most interesting type of work available with any of the so-called "service" stipends.

Ordinarily, an RA is paid from a grant that has been

awarded a particular faculty member. Since it is the faculty member's grant, he will decide on who is hired as "his" RA as well as what work is done by that person.

Beyond the obvious advantage of doing interesting work, it is not uncommon for an RA's pay to continue through the summer months. True, the RA works for it but at least he's working at something with slightly more relevance to his life than selling hamburgers.

An RA may not be given waivers of tuition or fees as might a TA even though an RA is more likely to be doing the kind of work graduate study is supposed to teach. I believe this is because a TA is considered a sort of employee who is deserving of a slight discount. That sounds absolutely mad, I know, but there's no explanation for what happens when professional administrators and politicians make policy for universities.

Fellowship

This is probably the most common sort of aid offered to new graduate students. If you ever figured out what a scholarship is, then you know what a fellowship is. Supposedly, it's an award for academic merit that does not entail working at any job other than being a full-time graduate student.

If it should come down to your choice between an RAship and a fellowship in one of your target departments, take the RAship. A nonservice fellowship sounds very nice. Most students think they'll need to give their exclusive devotion to their course work but they're wrong. Graduate school is different in many ways from undergraduate school and this touches on one of the biggest differences. Generally speaking, graduate school is an apprentice system. You'll learn what's most valuable when you are doing with someone the things he knows how to

do. Whether that's research, or art, or thinking, the closer
you can come to being around when your teachers are doing what they do better than you do (not lecturing about
it), the better for you. A fellowship won't automatically get
you into that situation as will an RAship.

Fellowships are being based increasingly on the financial
need of the student to whom they're awarded. Since almost
all graduate students have some significant financial need,
this comes down to deciding who is in the most serious
need of aid. Academicians still cling strongly to the idea
that a nonservice fellowship should be partly based on
academic achievement or promise so simple poverty will
not assure you of such an award. Poverty and promise is
an unbeatable combination, though.

All institutions require students applying for aid to file a
separate application for this purpose. Some use their own
form, some require an application submitted through the
Graduate and Professional School Financial Aid Council,
and some a form submitted through the College Scholarship Service (CSS). These last two are creatures of the
Educational Testing Service (Princeton, New Jersey), the
same outfit that operates the Graduate Records Examination. The Aid Council's form is known as GAPSFAS (the
last S stands for "service" which suggests one or two amusing images); the CSS's form is know as FAF (standing,
simply enough, for Financial Aid Form). Strictly speaking,
the GAPSFAS was created for use by graduate student applicants while the FAF was for undergraduate applicants.
Still, many graduate schools require the FAF alone since,
one assumes, it's easier to use one form for all students.

Both the GAPSFAS and the FAF require that you provide information about your own assets and debts, those
of your spouse, and those of your parents or guardians.
The GAPSFAS even requires such information about your

spouse-to-be if you're planning to get married in the near future. Once you've submitted this form, a "need analysis" is made and that information is sent to schools you've designated. It costs you more and more money for each additional school you designate to receive your GAPSFAS (or FAF) analysis. The individual schools then make financial aid awards according to their own standards; you can get the required form somewhere on your own campus in an office of financial aid or of student affairs.

Treat any financial aid form as you would a coiled rattlesnake. You shouldn't lie but there's no reason to take an optimistic view of your financial circumstances either.

Even though the U.S. Constitution, federal statute, and probably the statutes in most states declare an individual who's over eighteen to be an independent legal entity, a given university may have a very different viewpoint. Both the GAPSFAS and FAF forms ask you to report whether, in the prior year, (1) you lived with your parents for more than two consecutive *weeks*, or (2) your parents contributed more than $600 toward your support. They also ask whether your parents counted you as a deduction on their federal income tax report in the prior two years. If any one of these things were true, you're required to include a detailed financial statement about your parents, certified by them to be correct.

You may plan to be on your own in graduate school (and you can say so on the form) but if ETS has its way, all of your financial obligations and assets (perhaps including your parents) will be weighed in the balance. I'll have more to say about establishing your legal independence when I discuss tuition and fee tricks.

Allow at least one month from the time ETS receives your application to the time your designated schools will receive your need analysis. Take that time period into consideration in relation to deadlines for filing financial aid applications in your target schools.

Minority Fellowship

If you are Black, Hispanic, American Indian, Asian, or a Pacific Islander, there are many fellowships for which you will be eligible.

As a prospective graduate student you should check your target schools in a book titled *Graduate and Professional School Opportunities for Minority Students* which is published by the Educational Testing Service (Princeton, New Jersey). This book will give you the name and address of an individual on each campus to contact. Write this person and ask about financial aid.

In fact, write this person before doing anything else in connection with graduate application. Realism is realism. I don't believe you will find it necessary to manage your impression as diligently as would a nonminority individual. Minority students are in great demand at universities everywhere. Just let them know you're interested in coming to graduate school.

If you'll register with the Minority Graduate Student Locator Service of the Educational Testing Service (Princeton, New Jersey), you'll be contacted by schools interested in increasing their enrollment of minority students. There is no charge for this registration; ask someone on your campus about it.

Independent Fellowships

These are fellowships granted qualified students who have applied directly to the federal, state, or private agency that sponsors the fellowship. Once received, the student may attend any graduate school that will accept him.

Such a student is said to "bring his own money." Since

he won't cost the accepting department any of its own support funds, he is more likely to be accepted. Of course, if he has qualified for the fellowship primarily on academic merit (rather than because of his Civil War ancestry, for example) he is even more likely to be accepted wherever he applies.

The number of these fellowships has declined sharply as the Feds have increasingly restricted their direct support of graduate education. Check the financial guide for your field that I described in Chapter 2 for information about such fellowships as may exist when you're reading this book. Better still, check *The Grants Register* I'll cite later.

Work-Study

This is a form of hunting license that is sometimes granted new students. The money itself comes from a federal grant to the institution. The award is supposedly based entirely on financial need but so many graduate students will qualify on that basis that other factors (i.e., academic merit or specialized skills) will be very important.

A work-study grant is an authorization for you to earn a certain total amount at the local hourly rate for a semester, quarter, or term. Some institutions "provide" you with work to do; some leave it up to you to make a connection that you prefer and work at that.

When you have this sort of choice, you won't have difficulty finding some faculty member willing to put you to work on some facet of his research. Why should any be unwilling? They don't have to pay you. Almost any faculty member will be happy to be presented with the gift of your services. From your point of view, it's almost like an RAship. It doesn't pay as much but it puts you in touch with research work and makes acquaintances among the faculty. If you're offered work-study money, it's a good idea to ask whether you'll have any choice about the kind of work you'll do.

Tuition/Fee Tricks

It is fairly common for TAs to be granted a waiver (or remission) of either their tuition, fees, or both. Some institutions also grant these waivers (or remissions) to new students awarded other kinds of aid or, even, no other aid.

A waiver means that you aren't asked to pay the tuition or fee in question. A remission is little more than a book-keeper's trick from your point of view. A remission means that the school gives you the required money in some form that you can't spend for anything else. Then you pay the tuition or fee by giving back this otherwise nonnegotiable play money. As you can guess, that means just one more line in which you'll be forced to stand during registration.

If you are going to another state, and the out-of-state tuition is high, a tuition waiver or remission can be a life-saver. So, if tuition is an important piece of money at one of your target schools, ask about waivers or remissions before deciding whether other aid they've offered you has any meaning. It won't do you much good if Allamagoosa U. offers a $1,500 fellowship and later makes you pay $1,700 per year in tuition and fees because you're an out-of-state resident. It's very hard to live on minus $200.

As a new graduate student—old enough to be an independent legal entity—you almost certainly can find some way to limit payment of the out-of-state tuition to two semesters. For example, a great many universities define an in-state resident for graduate school purposes as one who pays some tax in the state, or who is registered to vote in the state, or both.

Consequently, look into these rules for your target schools. By amendment to the U.S. Constitution, you are eligible to register to vote in federal elections in pretty much any town you choose to call home. If that will qualify you for in-state tuition, plan to register to vote as soon as you arrive if there's no waiver or remission of the out-of-state portion of the tuition. If paying taxes will qualify you, ask whether a personal property tax is charged on cars registered in the state. Then plan to register your car there and count the $30-$50 annual tax on it money well spent for as long as you stay at that school without an out-of-state tuition waiver. The graduate school catalog or bulletin for each school will tell you how an in-state student is defined.

Another trick that you should know has to do with tuition or fee deferment. Suppose you've been awarded a $2,000 fellowship. These awards are usually paid in a lump sum near the beginning of the academic year (which event may teach you more about budgeting your money than you really want to know). However, you might learn that registration occurs before you are likely to receive your fellowship check and fear not having enough money on hand to pay your tuition and fees when you register. If so, contact the graduate school or office of financial aid before you arrive, and ask if you can arrange for a deferment of payment until you have your fellowship money. The idea to accept is that if you have this problem, scores of students before you have had it. Some mechanism for bridging this temporary gap is, therefore, very likely to exist, and you should feel free to ask about it. Don't expect to get a deferment for more than a month or two, but if you have a reasonable case to present you probably can expect that period of postponement of payment.

Loan Authorization

This form of aid is awarded you by a school but it comes down to permitting you to borrow a certain amount of money (depending on your need analysis) each year. As with any loan, you'll be required to agree to repay this money on some fixed schedule at some interest charge.

The big difference between these loans and those you might arrange on your own is that the repayment schedule will let you finish school before you begin repayment. Moreover, these loans (usually guaranteed by the Feds or by a state) entail miniscule interest rates that you'd never get on your own.

The so-called NDSL (National Direct Student Loans) is the best known of this type. It is quite possible that if you attend a public university there will be a state program (e.g., the Guaranteed Student Loan Program [GSLP]) from which you can borrow as much as $2,500 per year. For the GSLP you must get an application from a local bank, complete it, and send it to the school in which you're enrolled. That school validates your application and returns it to the bank; the bank then loans you as much as its own standards dictate.

With the GSLP, you must actually be enrolled in some graduate school before you know how much money you'll be able to borrow. That's not much help to an applicant who is trying to decide where to attend school. With the NDSL, the department knows how much you'll qualify to borrow before it makes the offer to you. Still, you can complete a GSLP form and visit your local bank to see if an officer is willing to make a guess at how much money you might borrow if you were enrolled in graduate school. He may waffle but it doesn't hurt to ask.

The big advantage of GSLP is that you can decide which school to attend and then have an independent source of financial aid once you're there. It's not quite like bringing your money with you as you can with a few fellowships that are awarded by some foundations. But it's close, and frees you to decide where to go without being tied to questions of what you'll go on.

Traineeships

These are programs supported by the Feds or by industrial groups for the training of certain sorts of graduate students. The traineeship, where it exists, will pay a student a nonservice stipend for a guaranteed four- or five-year period as long as he is making satisfactory progress toward a Ph.D. in a specified area. These plums are awarded by the department since the department has, itself, applied or arranged for some number of traineeships directly with the sponsoring agency for, say, a five-year period.

If there is an industrial sponsor of a trainee program, there may very well be a guaranteed summer job in that industry for the students who hold traineeships. Since these jobs are in the field being studied, that is a very nice way to learn while paying the summer rent.

Bringing Your Own Money

Almost all graduate students receive whatever financial aid they get through their graduate department or school. The money involved originates from the federal government, the state government, or wealthy benefactors living and dead. But it goes to the school first, and is then distributed in several different ways and forms to the student recipients. None of the recipients at a given school would be eligible for that school's money unless they were enrolled there.

If you had an independent source of money, you'd have,

among other things, much greater freedom to decide where to attend. Wealthy relatives would do, but if you haven't those, you should consider applying for your own "grant" money. Then you could take it with you to whatever school you decide to attend.

This sort of money is awarded by a variety of public and private agencies. The source to use in learning more about the grants, who's eligible, and where to write for applications is titled *The Grants Register*. A new edition appears every two years; it's published by St. Martins Press in New York. It's primarily intended for students at or above the graduate level or for those seeking further professional or vocational training.

The granting agencies will probably request your *hard* and *soft* credentials as a part of your application. The work you do to cultivate strong *soft credentials* for your regular application to graduate school will benefit you just as much in making a grant application.

Closing dates are often early in the calendar year. Check the most recent edition of *The Grants Register* in your reference library.

Your Shots Echo

It can be a fairly grim experience to await some echoing response from the schools to which you've applied. But, that's only if you wait, holding your breath and sitting by the telephone.

My advice is to recognize that there are two bench marks in your campaign. The first is reached when all the papers your target departments require have been submitted. The second is not reached until you're sure each target department has accepted every last one of its new students (if you're not one of them). Your campaign should continue beyond the completion of your application.

As my earlier discussion of identity-building argued, you

should not take a passive attitude while waiting for an echo. Telephone calls for various reasons, letters inquiring about reprints, copies of papers to be added to your file, and personal visits to the campus are all advisable during this period of your campaign. Keep your name, interests, and existence alive in the minds of your gatekeepers. This cannot hurt you if you're polite about it and it shows exactly the kind of initiative your gatekeepers want to find in their students.

It is quite common for students to draw all sorts of ego-damaging inferences from any delays in responses from their target departments. The first question to consider, then, is whether these responses are "delayed." Academicians do not look forward to reading applications and they often put it off as long as circumstances permit.

There are customs and pressures which exist in different fields that do make it possible for someone who knows a field to identify its general recruitment schedule. Such a person is your *tipster* or advisor. Once they've written their letters of recommendation for you there's no reason to avoid questioning them. You needn't defend your image with someone whose opinion no longer makes any difference in your campaign.

Unless your *tipster* has actually worked in one of your target departments, he probably won't know exactly when things happen there on admissions. Still, he'll know whether block or rolling admissions are customary, and approximately when first-round acceptances are probably offered.

I've described block admissions earlier so I'll only add that rolling admission refers to the practice of immediately considering an application whenever it arrives. A rolling admission is most likely to be used if there are fewer applicants than desired. There's probably some reason for that, by the way, so if confronted with a rolling admissions practice, check to see if the reason makes any difference to you.

As I've mentioned earlier, the typical procedure of deciding on admissions will result in a pool of first-round applicants and a pool of second-round applicants. Just because you might be in the second-round pool doesn't mean your target department doesn't want you. (There's another untitled pool in most academic fields; that's the pool of applicants which a particular department does not want to accept.) If all first-round applicants go elsewhere, departments will almost surely be prepared to accept some number of applicants in the second-round pool.

You are probably so accustomed to thinking of yourself in terms of a GPA or a class rank in comparison to other students, that it's understandably difficult for you to accept that graduate students simply are not chosen by such strict one-dimensional standards. A student applying to one department of biology might be accepted with a lower GPA than another student applying to the same department. Your *hard credentials* do make a difference in the acceptance decision but if your interests mesh with those of faculty in a particular department you might be chosen over another student with "better" *hard credentials*. For this same reason, you might be accepted by a *maximum class* department but not be accepted by a *middle class* department. It depends on what sort of person you seem to be in relation to what sorts of people are in a given graduate department.

It is even possible that you'll be considered a *nochance applicant*—someone whose credentials are so good that you'll never actually come even if accepted. Academicians know all about insurance schools, too.

If you want to avoid beign treated as a *nochance applicant* by any department you must make a special effort to
describe your interests as fitting very closely with the particular faculty in that department. If you provide sufficient
detail on this point in your autobiographical statement,
you can convince them that this is a reason for your unexpected interest in their department.

Once that's done, they'll be delighted to put you at the
top of their list. This will provide you with the insurance
that you surely had in mind when you applied to this
school.

A Last Encouraging Word

Except for the epilogue this brings me to the end.

I know you're better prepared for applying yourself now
than 99 percent of your compatriots-in-application. I hope
you believe that, too.

Whether or not you do believe now, let me share with
you one last truth about human beings. If you act as if you
know what you're doing, no one will doubt that you do
without a lot of contradictory evidence.

Epilogue

One of the realities you'll face when you complete your graduate degree is the job market. You may be aiming at an academic job of some kind (over 65 percent of all Ph.D.'s work in an educational institution), or one in industry, or commerce, or a government agency. Whichever it is, the supply of people with your degree in relation to the demand in a particular sector is the only supply and demand that matters to you.

Future, Not Past

You will hear some gloom and doom from the academicians who are on the faculty of your department about how terrible things are "these days." To those people, things are terrible compared to, say, the early sixties but that is utterly irrelevant to your circumstances.

Your Life Goes Forward

Whatever the employment market is in the present and near future, the past is not your concern. It's gone. What would the faculty have you do—stop the world and get off until things change? They sometimes sound as if that's what they're saying but they are merely talking as all human beings talk when they wish the good old days were here again. Have you ever stopped to consider that your present and near future will be someone's "good old days" twenty years from now? So, as a realist, cope with what faces you but don't take on a burden of discouragement because you face a reality different from that which is now gone.

Degrees Are An Edge

Whatever the state of employment supply and demand, you'll have a broader range of job opportunities with a graduate degree than without one. Approximately thirty thousand new *junior* faculty members per quinquennium (How's that for a "larger word"? It means five-year period) will be needed to *replace* older faculty who die or retire between 1976 and 1990. Only people with graduate degrees will be eligible for those jobs. Why shouldn't you plan to be the person who gets one of them?

Aside from that, as the supply of job applicants becomes large relative to the supply, employers tend to raise the entrance qualifications for jobs. When employers find they have more applicants than jobs, a job that would have once required a B.A. degree among applicants is likely to have its description rewritten to require a master's degree. If you have the higher degree, you will be eligible for the newly described job.

Then, too, as Cartter wrote, "Ph.D.'s have many alternative employment opportunities outside of higher education. Thus, unemployment is seldom the fate of a person holding the highest earned degree, although he or she may face short-term unemployment during a job search" (Cartter (1976), p. 187; see An Obscure Appendix).

Getting Ready for It

Since you've decided to go to graduate school, there are actions you can take while you're there to enhance your chances of getting the job you want after you complete your degree. These include multiplication of general-purpose skills which you acquire while you're doing your degree studies. I'll say more about this subject shortly.

Projections about the Future

I've listed for you the best available sources of estimates of the future employment market (see An Obscure Appendix following). I've leaned on several of these sources for what I'll say here but the advantage for you in examining the publications of the Bureau of Labor Statistics (BLS) is that they are updated periodically. Look for the most recent BLS bulletins when you're doing your own planning.

If you've already decided what you're going to be, these projections won't (and probably shouldn't) affect your decision. Still, there is a degree of substitutibility between law and social science, medicine and life science, business and public administration that might permit you to make some shifts in your plans if the employment projections seem to you to warrant that.

Don't take these projections for more than they are. They are informed estimates based on a number of assumptions about the shape of the future given the shape of the past. Unexpected factors can transform these projections into very inaccurate predictions.

You won't remember it personally but you may have heard about what happened to the field of engineering after Russia surprised the world with Sputnik I. That first-ever orbiting Russian satellite sent the United States government into a frenzy of financial support for anything connected with space flight. The engineering schools boomed for years, jobs for engineers were everywhere, and the National Aeronautics and Space Administration (NASA) commands a fairly heavy piece of government funds to this day.

Anyone who published projections of future employment for engineers in 1956 before the "beep" heard (literally) around the world was very far off the mark. But, as always, I counsel looking at the way things are or will be as realistically as you can see or discover. As I said in the preface, eyes open is better than eyes closed any day.

According to BLS (Bulletin 1860), the need for Ph.D.'s in the period 1972 to 1985 would grow about 50 percent more than that of all workers. By 1985, the employment needs requirements for Ph.D.'s were projected to have increased to 475,000 from the estimated 335,000 employed Ph.D.'s in 1972.

This Ph.D. employment need however, was expected to grow more slowly from 1972 to 1985 than the need for what BLS calls "college educated" workers. This category includes those with two-year, four-year, and masters degrees as well as those who've gone to college but completed no degree. By comparison, the employment need for college-educated workers was projected to grow 75 percent more than for Ph.D. workers and about 150 percent more than for all workers over the 1972-to-1985 period.

Some BLS projections also deal with specific fields and the estimated supply and demand in each (BLS Bulletin 1918). Much more detailed area information is presented in these bulletins than I'll mention here.

At the Ph.D. degree level, though, the largest percentage

increase in employment need relative to the base employment in 1974 was expected in psychology (76 percent); engineering (59 percent), and the life sciences (32 percent) by 1985. The three fields in which the smallest percentage increases in need were expected were the arts/humanities (−2 percent), physics (5 percent), and business (5 percent).

Perhaps a more practical view of projections in various fields is that which compares the percentage of projected Ph.D. supply and job openings *over* the 1974−1985 period. I've derived these percentages from Bulletin 1918 and shown them in Figure 4.

Figure 4
Projections for Ph.D.'s

Field	New Supply, 1974-85	Openings, 1974-85	% Supply of Openings
Engineering	29,100	30,300	96%
Chemistry	18,000	14,200	127%
Physics	12,100	6,600	183%
Life Sciences	59,500	33,600	177%
Mathematics	12,400	5,900	210%
Social Science	50,700	20,900	243%
Psychology	38,100	27,500	139%
Arts/Humanities	52,600	9,100	578%
Education	115,400	35,200	328%
Business/Commerce	13,300	1,600	831%
Other	13,300	3,600	369%

Note. Projections assume a small continuing growth in the proportion of Ph.D.'s in each occupation. Adapted from Table 13, p.21 (BLS Bulletin 1918).

A percentage greater than 100 percent signifies greater projected supply than openings during the 1974 to 1985 period.

The only field in which there was expected to be a greater supply of openings than Ph.D.'s was engineering. You might think of those percentages in the right-hand column of Figure 4 as reflecting the number of applicants per 100 openings. In psychology, there was projected to be 139 new Ph.D.'s for each 100 openings or, about 1.4 new Ph.D.'s per opening. Compared with the approximately 6 new Ph.D.'s per opening in the arts/humanities that seems almost bearable.

None of these projections allow very adequately for Ph.D.'s in the period who might become employed in areas not previously drawing Ph.D. workers. Operating crystal balls are in very short supply and no one can make solid allowances for that sort of response to tight employment markets or to unexpected techological developments.

However, since the largest proportion of Ph.D.'s will probably continue to work in educational institutions, it's worth looking at the shape of things there in particular. The boom years for employment of academic Ph.D.'s were most recently in the early to middle sixties. This resulted from a number of pressures working together (earlier baby booms, satellites, and such). One lasting effect as far as you're concerned is that a lot of faculty were hired then who won't begin retiring until sometime between 1995 and 2000. This, coupled with the *relatively* fewer children born following the World War II baby boom and the tenure practices of most educational institutions, means that colleges are staffed to deal with large numbers of students though the number of students is declining. And, that means a relative decline in numbers of new faculty needed even though the supply of new Ph.D.'s will probably remain high. Those boom babies do grow up and many go on to get a Ph.D. degree.

Allan Cartter, the same man who headed the 1964

survey of the quality of graduate education I mentioned in chapter 2, worked from data available in 1972 but concerned himself exclusively with the academic Ph.D. labor market. I've compared some of his projections with data that have become available since his study and he was generally not far off the mark. The further into the future anything gets, the more wobble there will be in estimating it.

Cartter's estimate of the demand for new junior faculty in the future (including both replacement and growth needs) is for about 68,000 from 1976 to 1980, 22,000 from 1981 to 1985, 22,000 from 1986 to 1990, 18,000 from 1991 to 1995, and, then, 85,000 for the period from 1996 to 2000. These are *totals* for successive five-year periods; the *annual* hirings of new junior faculty between 1962 and 1972 averaged about 27,000.

It's against the memory of that sort of annual average which your graduate school teachers will compare "these days." Still, their past is entirely irrelevant to your future. And, as I said earlier, there are some special things I believe you can do while in graduate school to prepare to cope with your own world of the future.

Skills Galore

As you now think of it, a master's or Ph.D. degree will qualify you for jobs unobtainable by a very large percentage of the population. You're correct. A graduate degree will do that.

However, when you seek a job you won't be competing with a random selection of people from the population. Almost all of your competitors will have the same degree you hold. The same is true—even though degrees as such may not be involved—for any job you seek.

Your degree qualifies you to get into the competition for

the job but it doesn't guarantee you'll get the job when supply exceeds demand. Some degrees are "more equal" than others as my entire discussion of the role of the class of graduate departments should have made clear. But, even then, that's only true for those holding a given degree from different classes of departments who are in competition for exactly the same job.

For those holding degrees from the same class of graduate department, any competitive edge will arise from the unique qualifications of one or more of the applicants. I cannot say what unique qualifications you should seek to acquire because I don't know in what field you will hold your degree. Your *tipster* will know, though, and, later, your graduate advisor as well as other graduate students will know or help you come to know.

In psychology, for example, I'd advise any prospective student to lose no time in taking courses in computer programming, statistics, survey design, evaluation research, and writing. All of these would provide some experience with skills that have potential use in both academic and nonacademic settings. This course of action may improve the chances of getting an academic job if that's what's desired (remember those employers who multiply entry requirements in an oversupplied market). It may provide qualifications for a nonacademic job that others with the same degree will not have acquired. It may even provide employment in a field other than psychology (e.g., computer programming) for a few years until the demand for psychologists increases.

Whatever it does, having skills galore will never hurt and will probably help. Just because your graduate teachers do not have, have never needed, or do not want to have a variety of skills with nonacademic application is no reason to model yourself entirely on them. They don't live in your employment world. If they'd object, just don't tell 'em and go right ahead to get ready for your own future.

I wish you all the good fortune that you deserve. But, don't count on luck. Count on realistic planning.

An
Obscure Appendix

Some might call this a bibliography. They'd be wrong. A bibliography cites works for background or further reading and no one should think of actually reading the sources I've cited here. Consulting, yes, but not reading.

Some might call it a reference list but they'd be wrong, too. I didn't refer to all these works in support of points that I made. Rather, I've listed them here so that you may refer to them in making points. There's a big difference.

So, with the thought that no realist would care what I called this section, I decided on An Obscure Appendix. It has a certain bluntness about it that appealed to me.

Academic Turfs

1. *The Annual Guide to Graduate Study.* Peterson's Guides, Inc. Multiple volumes; annual editions. This is your *program.*
2. *An Assessment of Qualilty in Graduate Education.*

Allan Cartter. American Council on Education, 1966. This is *not* your *playbook*.

3. *Barron's Guide to Graduate Schools.* Barron's Education Series, Inc. Only Volume 1, "The Social Sciences and Psychology," is published; five additional volumes on other clusters of fields are planned.

4. *The College Blue Book: Degrees Offered by College and Subject.* Macmillan Publishing Co. Periodic editions.

5. *The College Blue Book: Narrative Descriptions.* Macmillan Publishing Co. Periodic editions.

6. *The College Blue Book: Tabular Data.* Macmillan Publishing Co. Periodic editions.

7. *Graduate and Professional School Opportunities for Minority Students.* Educational Testing Service. Periodic editions.

8. *Graduate Programs and Admissions Manual.* Multiple volumes; GPAM lists program guides prepared by national associations. Annual.

9. *A Guide to Graduate Study: Programs Leading to the Ph.D. Degree.* American Council on Education. Periodic editions.

10. *A Rating of Graduate Programs.* Kenneth Roose and Charles Anderson. American Council on Education, 1970. This *is* your *playbook*.

Index Periodicals: Academic Publications

1. *ABC Pol Sci: Advance Bibliography of Contents.* Santa Barbara, California: American Bibliographical Center, Clio Press. An author and subject citation index (no abstracts) to the periodical literature in political science, government, sociology, law, and economics. Five issues a year.

2. *Abstracts of English Studies.* Boulder, Colorado: National Council of Teachers of English. An author citation and abstract publication. Ten issues a year.
3. *Accountants' Index Supplement.* J. Kubat, ed. New York: American Institute of Certified Public Accountants, Inc. An author citation index (no abstracts) of English language publications on accounting. Three issues a year.
4. *The American Humanities Index.* Troy, New York: The Whitston Pub. Co. An author citation index covering over 250 creative and critical journals. Annual.
5. *Annual Science Citation Index.* Philadelphia, Pennsylvania: Institute for Science Information. The *Source Index* of this yearly *cumulative* index (no abstracts) is an author alphabetical listing. Annual.
6. *Applied Science and Technology Index.* The H. W. Wilson Co. A subject/author citation index (no abstracts). Annual.
7. *Art Index.* The H. W. Wilson Co. An author and subject citation index (no abstracts) to United States and foreign art periodicals and museum bulletins. Subject areas include archaeology, architecture, art history, arts and crafts, city planning, fine arts, graphic arts, industrial arts, interior design, landscape design, photography and films, and some related fields. Quarterly.
8. *Book Review Digest.* The H. W. Wilson Co. See chapter three.
9. *Book Review Index.* Detroit, Michigan: Gale Research Co. A *cumulative* author citation index (no abstracts) of 270 periodicals. Some periodical titles are: *American Anthropologist, Journal of Economic*

History, Modern Philology, Psychology Today, Yale Review. Bimonthly.

10. *Business Periodicals Index.* Bettie Jane Third, ed. The H. W. Wilson Co. An author citation index (no abstracts) of book reviews. Also, a subject/author citation index (no abstracts) of other publications during period covered. Annual.

11. *Combined Retrospective Index to Journals in History 1838—1974.* Arlington, Virginia: Carrollton Press, Inc., 1977. A nine-volume subject/author citation index (no abstracts) for domestic and foreign journals on United States and world history. Not a serial publication.

12. *Crime and Justice Abstracts.* Hackensack, New Jersey: National Council on Crime and Deliquency. A subject/author citation and abstract with no cumulation. The title was changed from *Crime and Delinquency Literature* in 1977. Annual.

13. *Current Book Review Citations.* The H. W. Wilson Co. See chapter 3.

14. *Film Literature Index.* Albany, New York: Filmdex, Inc. Author index (no abstracts) to the international film literature appearing in over 300 periodicals. Quarterly.

15. *Humanities Index.* The H. W. Wilson Co. An author and subject index (no abstracts) to periodicals in the fields of archaeology, classical studies, folklore, history, language and literature, literary and political criticism, performing arts, philosophy, religion and theology, and some related subjects. Quarterly.

16. *An Index to Book Reviews in the Humanities.* Williamston, Michigan: Phillip Thomson. A citation index alphabetical by author of the book reviewed

but including name of reviewer in easily visible location. Annual.

17. *Index to Book Reviews in Historical Periodicals.* J. W. Brewster and J. A. McLeod, eds. Metuchen, New Jersey: The Scarecrow Press, Inc. Author and citation index of book reviews (no excerpts) of English-language articles with most emphasis on United States history. Annual.

18. *International Bibliography of the Social Sciences.* Chicago: Aldine Publishing Co. Author and subject index (no abstracts) for all major domestic and foreign journals relating to sociology. Annual.

19. *MLA International Bibliography of Books and Articles on the Modern Languages and Literatures.* The Modern Language Association. An author and subject citation index (no abstracts) that is unusual in covering books, serial books, and journals. Annual; each of three volumes covers one broad topic area.

20. *The New York Times Book Review 1896–1970.* The New York Times, Inc. An author, subject, title, category, and byline citation index for books reviewed in the weekly *New York Times Book Review.* This is a five-volume set; the author volume is an index to the authors of the books reviewed while the by-line volume is an index to the authors of those reviews. Not a serial publication.

21. *Personnel Management Abstracts.* Ann Arbor; Michigan: University of Michigan Graduate School of Business Administration. An author, subject, and abstract citation index. Quarterly.

22. *The Philosopher's Index.* Bowling Green, Ohio: Philosophy Documentation Center, Bowling Green University. An author, subject, abstract index to the

major philosophy journals in English, French, German, Spanish, and Italian. Quarterly.

23. *The Philosopher's Index: A Retrospective Index to U.S. Publications from 1940.* Bowling Green, Ohio: Philosophy Documentatin Center, Bowling Green University. An author and subject citation index to philosophical books and journals from 1940 to 1978. It contains abstracts of some of the longer works. This is a three-volume set; volumes I and II are subject indices while volume III is an author index.

24. *Sage Race Relations Abstracts.* Beverly Hills, California: Sage Publications Inc. A subject/author and abstract citation index. Each issue also contains one extensive literature review on a relevant subject that is prepared by the Sage search staff. Quarterly.

25. *Sage Urban Studies Abstracts.* Beverly Hills, California: Sage Publications Inc. A subject/author and abstract citation index to relevant books, articles, pamphlets, government publications, speeches, and legislative research studies. Quarterly.

26. *Social Sciences Citation Index.* Philadelphia, Pennsylvania: The Institute for Science Information.

27. *Social Sciences Index.* The H. W. Wilson Co. A subject/author citation index (no abstracts) covering the major journals in anthropology, area studies, economics, environmental science, geography, law and criminology, medical science, political science, psychology, public administration, sociology, and some related fields. This title was changed from *Social Sciences and Humanities Index* in 1974. Annual.

28. *Science Citation Index.* Philadelphia, Pennsylvania: The Institute for Science Information.

29. *Women's Studies Abstracts.* Palmyra, New York: Rush Publishing Co. An author and abstract index to book reviews and articles. Quarterly.

Some Name Directories

In addition to names you'll find by using this list, directories of members are published by national professional associations. Some are no more than name and address listings but some contain a short biography on each individual. Your reference librarian can help you find the directory for your field.

The *Biographical Dictionaries Master Index* listed below is the first you should consult. If any gatekeeper is included in almost any biographical directory other then one published by a professional association, you'll almost certainly locate him with the BDMI.

1. *American Men and Women of Science.* Jaques Cattell Press. Periodic editions.

2. *Biographical Dictionaries Master Index.* D. LaBeau and G. Tarbert, eds. Gale Research Co. First edition, 1975; biennial editions are planned. A guide to more than 725,000 listings in over fifty current *Who's Who*s and other collective biographies.

3. *Directory of American Scholars.* Jaques Cattell Press. Periodic editions.

4. *The National Faculty Directory.* Gale Research Co. Annual. Contains names and addresses of about 500,000 teaching faculty in United States junior colleges through universities.

5. *Who's Who in American Art.* Jaques Cattell Press. Periodic editions.

6. *Who's Who in American Education.* R. Cook, ed. Who's Who in American Education, Inc. Biennial

editions. Contains bibliographic directory of university and college professors as well as others in the education business.

Money

All national professional associations give special attention to information about money for graduate student support. Consult the guide (listed in GPAM under Academic Turfs) published by the national association in your field.

1. *The Annual Register of Grant Support.* Marquis Who's Who, Inc. Biennial editions.
2. *Graduate and Professional School Opportunities for Minority Students.* Educational Testing Service. Periodic editions.
3. *The Grants Register.* St. James Press. Biennial editions.
4. *Guide to Financial Aid for Students in Arts and Sciences for Graduate and Professional Study.* Arco Publishing Co. Periodic editions.

Prep Books

1. *Graduate Record Examination Aptitude Test.* Arco Publishing Co. Periodic editions. This volume deals with the GRE VERBAL and GRE QUANTITATIVE parts of the examination. There are about twenty GRE-related Arco volumes. Each one is devoted to the GRE ADVANCED part of the examination in a particular field (e.g., "Psychology: Advanced Test for the G.R.E.," "Chemistry: Advanced Test for the G.R.E.," and "Biology: Advanced Test for the G.R.E.").
2. *How to Prepare for the MAT—Miller Analogies Test.* Barron's Publishing Service. Periodic editions. Barron's also publishes *prep books* on the Graduate

Management Admissions Test (GMAT), the Law School Admissions Test (LSAT), the Medical College Admissions Test (MCAT), and the Veterinarians College Admissions Test (VCAT). It nearly surpasses belief.

Futures

1. *Occupational Projections and Training Data.*Bureau of Labor Statistics, 1976. BLS Bulletin 1918. Periodic revisions.
2. *Ph.D. Manpower: Employment Demand and Supply, 1972–1985.* Bureau of Labor Statistics, 1975. BLS Bulletin 1860. Revised triennially.
3. *Ph.D.'s and the Academic Labor Market.* Allan M. Cartter. McGraw-Hill Book Co., 1976.
4. *Projections of Degrees and Enrollments in Science and Engineering Fields to 1985.* National Science Foundation. NSF document #76-301.
5. *Projections of Science and Engineering Doctorate Supply and Utilizations, 1980 and 1985.* National Science Foundation. NSF document #75-301.

Glossary

Area Shift. This is a plan by which you first adjust the area of study in which you apply to realistically fit the credentials you'll present. After acceptance to graduate school, you may shift your area of study to an allied area in a higher-class department at the same school on the basis of newly obtained graduate credentials.

Beatified. An applicant described in a letter of recommendation as (a) the best encountered in twenty years, (b) the sole hope for the future of the academic field in question, or (c) able to leap tall buildings in a single bound. No one actually believes any of these exaggerated claims by the letter writer, but they do draw gatekeepers' attention to the applicant.

Big Frog. An academician who has accomplished little and done so in the most self-aggrandizing manner possible but has, at most, a local reputation.

Big Name. An academician who is known to many for having accomplished much—whether or not many could
say exactly what that was.

Blanded. An applicant who is described in twenty-five
words or less and recommended without adjectival
enthusiasm for acceptance to graduate school or for
financial aid.

Boundary Spanner. A student whose credentials are inter-
nally inconsistent. This may reflect either an absence
of realistic advice or dramatic swings in academic
motivation.

Brag Sheet. A one-page promotional flyer on graduate
sub-areas, degrees offered, types of financial aid,
facilities, and faculty in an individual department.
Bulletin boards in office buildings on campuses are
thick with them; they're sent to applicants, colleagues, or anyone else who might have any reason to
want them. They almost always indicate the graduate-
degree school of each faculty member as well as his
sub-area of interest.

Career Credit. In the simplest terms, these are credits
leading to promotion, tenure, pay raises, and special
treatment as to teaching load and class hours. These
credits result from doing a lot of the sort of thing that
other academicians in one's field think to be really important. In research universities or colleges these
credits arise primarily from publication activity. In
nonresearch colleges, these credits do not arise,
primarily, from teaching activities as one might suppose. Anyone can lecture a class but it takes a different talent to win committee meetings, and that's
where the career credits are up for grabs.

Clubperson. An academician who is accorded claim to formal or informal membership in a given academic cli-

que. A clique may consist of those with common training, common activities, or common economic interests.

Clubspeak. The myriad bits of jargon—consisting of abbreviated words or phrases, technical designations, and allusions to common activities—that mark membership in any club with more than two human members. It's also human to think of all *clubspeak* as an affectation because we each only notice its use among members of clubs to which we do not belong. Our own clubs, or course, speak in language anyone can understand.

Comer Name. A young academician who is in the process of doing everything *big names* could claim to have done already if it weren't being described in a new clubspeak that the older academicians don't grasp entirely.

Credential Claims. These are your interpretations of your *hard* and *soft credentials*. You should accentuate the positive and avoid drawing attention to the negative. Your gatekeepers can read; let them find the negatives for themselves if they care to look.

Ex-Big Name. A *big name* who has not published for at least five years, has not been the president of a regional association (at least) for ten years and, moreover, doesn't care who knows it.

Festschrift. A collection of papers written by various *big names* and dedicated to the honor or memory of an *ex-big name* (usually deceased).

Gatekeeper. An academician who, knowingly or not, stands between the pasture you occupy and the one you want to occupy. He may be a letter writer, a decision-maker in admissions or aid or a potential employer. The purpose of impression management is to put your gatekeepers where you want them. The best place to put them is where they are doing something for you which they think is (or, will be) doing something for themselves.

GRE Advanced. Variant form is GREA. The part of the Graduate Record Examination on which you will do well if you remember the material from the introductory course that you first took in your field in college.

GRE Quantitative. Variant form is GREQ. The part of the Graduate Record Examination that tests your memory of the lessons in elementary college algebra, geometry, and that set theory the New Mathematicians have been insisting was good for you all these years.

GRE Verbal. Variant form is GREV. The part of the Graduate Record Examination which tests your verbal skills with multiple-choice questions about words stripped from the very context that distinguishes a language from a code. Experience with crossword puzzles helps.

Hard Credentials. These are grade transcripts, test scores, and the recorded facts of your financial circumstances. Do not fool around with forgery or lying. Still, your credential claims should stress those views of your *hard credentials* that you prefer not to have overlooked.

Hotness. There are fads or cycles or waves of activity in academic areas (as there are anywhere) in which certain types of research, theory, art, or literature are seemingly occupying everyone's attention. Five years after the peak of *hotness,* it's often difficult to remember exactly what was so fascinating about it all. *Hotness* is what the *big names* first say it is and what *comer names* then prove it is.

House Journal. The journal of a professional association dealing primarily with the protection of the livelihoods to which members of the association have (or, would like to) become accustomed.

If Offer. "Since you're still interested in Wayback U., *if* you decide to attend it *might* be possible to offer you financial aid of one sort or another that is somewhere in the range of [half enough to three-quarters enough]. Of course, we would have to have your decision in the very near future." None of this will be committed to writing until you say you will come.

In Status. This status is mostly due to who the individual's friends are and whether they have high *recognition status*. The "old boy" network is still alive and well in Academia. There are more women in it these days but it's still in full operation.

Insurance School. A graduate school or department for which your *hard* and *soft credentials* are much stronger than those of a typical applicant. This is a place that you can be almost certain will accept you if all else fails.

Knowing the Score. Having knowledge of how things are done, who's really who in the field, what's happened recently in the relevant academic activity (e.g., research), the latest line on the Feds, who's where and who's changed departments recently, who's published what recently, and anecdotes of all varieties about the great and the near-great. The annual regional or national conventions of the associations in the field are the occasions for keeping up with changes in the score.

Lower Class school/department. The size of the faculty and facilities will not distinguish these schools from *middle class* schools. The total amount of annual federal grants awarded to all faculty will be less than to those in *middle class* schools. A department in a *no-class* school may achieve *lower class* status if it obtains at least (a) one *big name* who has worked for years in another higher-class department but has moved down to retire and still receive a salary, or (b) two *comer names* who organize conferences, become associate editors, and circulate regularly among other *comer names* on the committees of the national professional association. Rated "Adequate Plus" in your *playbook*.

M.A. Only Farm Club. A deparment that awards a master's degree as its highest degree in your field providing it awards Ph.D. degrees in other fields.

M.A. Only School. A school that awards a master's degree as its highest degree in all areas of graduate study available there. Such a restriction may be due to state statute, tradition, or finances.

Maximum Class school/department. The schools which are biggest in faculty, facilities, and federal grants. A department in a nonmaximum class school may itself achieve *maximum class* status if it attains a critical mass consisting of, at least, (a) three *big names* who have had many, many students through the years, or (b) four *comer names* who take turns organizing annual conferences on their home campus while one becomes an editor of a major journal in the field, and (c) many young faculty who sleep an average of four in twenty-four hours and spend the remaining hours doing some sort of publication-related work. Rated "Distinguished" or "Strong" in your *playbook*.

Maybe Big Name. A full professor in a sub-area of a target department who might or might not be a *big name*. A *tipster* will know for sure.

Middle Class school/department. The schools which are of intermediate size in faculty, facilities, and federal grants. A department in a school of less than this class may, itself, achieve at least *middle class* if it contains (a) two *big names* who have had many students in the past, or (b) three *comer* names who organize annual conferences while two of them become associate editors of major journals in the field, and (c) five faculty who actually manage to get their papers published regularly in some major journal. Rated "Good" in your *playbook*.

Nochance Applicant. An applicant whose credentials are so much better than those of a typical applicant that the department will not expect him to come even if accepted. He will, the department expects, surely be accepted by a higher *class* department and prefer to go there. Such an applicant must seem to have a special interest in what is actually an insurance department or no offer of finanical aid will be made.

No Class school/department. These schools have a small faculty and limited facilities; they receive relatively tiny amounts of federal dollars. If the library is smaller than the basketball arena, all of the administrators have reserved parking places but faculty members do not, and many faculty members share an office — it is probably a *no class* school. Not openly listed in your *playbook* as such but compare the list of schools surveyed with departments that are rated "Adequate Plus" or better. If the school was surveyed but not rated, the conclusion is obvious.

OK-Different. The *OK* refers to a dimension of approval while the *different* refers to a dimension of comparison with other people. Academicians approve of high standing on many dimensions of behavior in graduate students: seriousness, reliability, in-graduate students: seriousness, reliability, intelligence, deference, docility, maturity, articulateness, and so on. They also compare students they encounter with a mixed set of students they remember, students they hope to have and students they believe they encounter all the time. An *OK-different* student is one who is high on approved dimensions as compared with the students academicians believe they encounter all the time.

PAA. Preferred Academic Advisor. This is not *clubspeak*. I created PAA myself. Won't ma be astonished? Bad puns are endemic in Academia. If you can't abide them, keep it a secret or few will miss an opportunity to punish you with them. See?

Papertalk. Since publication plays such an important role in academicians' lives, it's understandable that their *clubspeak* would include words and phrases relating to this activity. Here are a few for your use. Don't overdo it.

—*in preparation*. A manuscript an academician is thinking of writing or is writing but which is not yet typed in final draft.

—*submitted* (or, under editorial consideration). A manuscript that has been mailed to an editor who has not yet rejected it.

—*in press*. A manuscript that has been accepted on condition of stipulated modifications, or is even beyond that stage but not yet actually published.

—*pre-print*. A manuscript that has been typed in final draft, copied, and is available for examination if not quotation.

—*re-print*. A printed copy of the paper as it was published.

—*manuscript* (or, MS; pronounced *em ess*, naturally). The typed copy of a paper, chapter, or book which may then be reproduced in various forms depending on the intended circulation.

— *reviewer* (or consultant or referee). An individual whom the editor believes is competent to review an MS and make a recommendation about publishing it. An author almost never knows a reviewer's identity.

— *blind review.* A reviewer is "blind" if he does not know the identity of the author of an MS he is reviewing. The point is to avoid the appearance of evil and, perhaps, even attain greater objectivity in reviews.

— *page charges.* Authors are not paid for their publications in even semireputable journals. In some fields, authors pay a fixed charge per page (often disguised as a reprint charge) for publication in both reputable and semireputable journals. In other fields, authors pay nothing for publication in noncommercial journals and, usually, are provided some number of reprints of their paper free of charge. In these fields, rejection rates are very high in freebie journals so page charges continue to be paid to semireputable journals.

— *galleys.* A very "in" word which refers to the preprinting copy (the first setting into type of an MS). This is usually the only copy sent an author for review (proofreading, mainly) before the paper, chapter, or book is actually printed. The *minimum* sequence is: (1) author sends MS, (2) editor accepts paper, (3) author receives, corrects, and returns galleys, and (4) journal number containing the paper is printed.

Preliminary List. A list of eight to twelve (and sometimes a few more) potential-target schools that are to be investigated in detail for use in collecting strong letters of recommendation or in making future applications.

Prep Book. A commercial publication designed for

preparation for one of the national examinations (GRE, MAT). The information these provide goes far beyond simple presentation of typical test items. See a sample listing in An Obscure Appendix of this book.

Puff Claims. An account of all varieties of faculty activities, honors, and grant awards. Nothing is too small to escape listing; budget money may be at stake.

Recognition Status. This status is mostly due to publications, prominence in national associations, and that sort of thing. Basically, however, this status derives from the simple frequency with which an individual's name reaches the eyes or ears of large numbers of colleagues. High *recognition status* comes from having a distinctive last name, publishing a lot, joining many associations, becoming some sort of editor of a journal in the field, organizing conferences or paper sessions at conventions, helping to found specialized societies of like-minded academic colleagues, and so on and on. Anything that gets the individual's name out in front where it can be seen often will serve to pump up this status.

Recspeak. The scores of coded phrases used in letters of recommendation to convey all degrees of enthusiasm from zero to near infinite.

Self-Classification. The act of seeing yourself through the same peepholes your gatekeepers will use.

Soft Credentials. These are letters of recommendation, statements of your interests or plans, and your estimates of the problematic elements of your future financial resources while in graduate school. Impression management is the key to accumulating strong *soft credentials* and arranging the most beneficial reaction to them.

Stepping Stones To Anywhere. This is a plan by which you first enter the highest class department obtainable by you in your area. After a year of study, you then transfer on the basis of newly obtained graduate credentials to another school having a higher class department in the area in which you began. After another year in the second school, you may repeat this transfer process to still another school. Anywhere is your destination.

Stud Book. Biographical directories in which minutiae of academic events in the lives of those listed are recorded for reference, posterity, and ego-tripping.

Sub-Area. A specialty within one of the traditional academic areas. Some areas still try to train graduate students broadly in all of the parts of the field but, particularly in larger departments, that has been abandoned. In the field of psychology, some lip service is still given, for example, to training "psychologists" but, other than a few required "breadth" courses, graduate students study to be clinical, developmental, physiological, comparative, social, personality, or linguistic psychologists these days. There's too much to learn in four to six years — or so it's thought — for students to try to learn it all.

Sub-Area Shift. This is a plan by which you first enter a department in a sub-area with relatively little competition from people with higher *classifications* than your own. After you've arrived, you begin arranging to shift from this sub-area to the sub-area in that department in which you were really interested all along. It works but don't neglect your impression management after you've arrived. That's why it works.

Tailored List. A short list of departments shown to a
   potential reference letter writer indicating (briefly)
   reasons for your interest in each department. These
   departments are not necessarily all of your final target
   departments. One of the departments on this list
   should be the one from which the gatekeeper who sees
   it received his own graduate degree.

Target Department. This is a department to which you actually apply for admission as a graduate student. You
   may not expect to go there if accepted (given another
   choice) or even expect to have your best chance to be
   accepted there (given an optimistic aim), but there's
   no reason anyone else need know either of these
   things.

Tipster. An approachable faculty member at a student's
   home school whose sub-area of interest is the same
   (or as close as possible) as that to which application is
   made for graduate study. A *tipster* may or may not be
   the student's academic advisor.

Transition Problem. The question of how what happened
   while you were an undergraduate could have possibly
   led to what you want to happen to you as a graduate
   student.

Validity Checks. These are actions by the source which
   originates some documentary part of your credentials
   to signify that the testament is historically accurate
   (i.e., valid). The embossed stamp on the copy of your
   official transcript sent by your undergraduate school
   to your target department is a validity check; it signifies that the recorded grades were those you received.
   There are similar validity checks on your GRE and
   MAT score reports.

Index

DATE DUE

APR 3 0 1981		
AUG 2 1 1987		
JUL 0 3 1992		
MAR 4		
OCT 2		
OCT		